New Directions for
Higher Education

Betsy O. Barefoot
Jillian L. Kinzie
Co-editors

Toward a Scholarship of Practice

John M. Braxton
Editor

Number 178 • Summer 2017
Jossey-Bass
San Francisco

Toward a Scholarship of Practice
John M. Braxton
New Directions for Higher Education, no. 178
Co-editors: *Betsy O. Barefoot and Jillian L. Kinzie*

NEW DIRECTIONS FOR HIGHER EDUCATION, (Print ISSN: 0271-0560; Online ISSN: 1536-0741), is published quarterly by Wiley Subscription Services, Inc., a Wiley Company, 111 River St., Hoboken, NJ 07030-5774 USA.

Postmaster: Send all address changes to NEW DIRECTIONS FOR HIGHER EDUCATION, John Wiley & Sons Inc., C/O The Sheridan Press, PO Box 465, Hanover, PA 17331 USA.

Information for subscribers
New Directions for Higher Education is published in 4 issues per year. Institutional subscription prices for 2017 are:
Print & Online: US$454 (US), US$507 (Canada & Mexico), US$554 (Rest of World), €363 (Europe), £285 (UK). Prices are exclusive of tax. Asia-Pacific GST, Canadian GST/HST and European VAT will be applied at the appropriate rates. For more information on current tax rates, please go to www.wileyonlinelibrary.com/tax-vat. The price includes online access to the current and all online back files to January 1st 2013, where available. For other pricing options, including access information and terms and conditions, please visit www.wileyonlinelibrary.com/access.

Delivery Terms and Legal Title
Where the subscription price includes print issues and delivery is to the recipient's address, delivery terms are **Delivered at Place (DAP)**; the recipient is responsible for paying any import duty or taxes. Title to all issues transfers FOB our shipping point, freight prepaid. We will endeavour to fulfil claims for missing or damaged copies within six months of publication, within our reasonable discretion and subject to availability.

Back issues: Single issues from current and recent volumes are available at the current single issue price from cs-journals@wiley.com.

Disclaimer
The Publisher and Editors cannot be held responsible for errors or any consequences arising from the use of information contained in this journal; the views and opinions expressed do not necessarily reflect those of the Publisher and Editors, neither does the publication of advertisements constitute any endorsement by the Publisher and Editors of the products advertised.

Publisher: New Directions for Student Leadership is published by Wiley Periodicals, Inc., 350 Main St., Malden, MA 02148-5020.

Journal Customer Services: For ordering information, claims and any enquiry concerning your journal subscription please go to www.wileycustomerhelp.com/ask or contact your nearest office.
Americas: Email: cs-journals@wiley.com; Tel: +1 781 388 8598 or +1 800 835 6770 (toll free in the USA & Canada).
Europe, Middle East and Africa: Email: cs-journals@wiley.com; Tel: +44 (0) 1865 778315.
Asia Pacific: Email: cs-journals@wiley.com; Tel: +65 6511 8000.
Japan: For Japanese speaking support, Email: cs-japan@wiley.com.
Visit our Online Customer Help available in 7 languages at www.wileycustomerhelp.com/ask

Production Editor: Poornita Jugran (email: pjugran@wiley.com).

Wiley's Corporate Citizenship initiative seeks to address the environmental, social, economic, and ethical challenges faced in our business and which are important to our diverse stakeholder groups. Since launching the initiative, we have focused on sharing our content with those in need, enhancing community philanthropy, reducing our carbon impact, creating global guidelines and best practices for paper use, establishing a vendor code of ethics, and engaging our colleagues and other stakeholders in our efforts. Follow our progress at www.wiley.com/go/citizenship

View this journal online at wileyonlinelibrary.com/journal/he

Wiley is a founding member of the UN-backed HINARI, AGORA, and OARE initiatives. They are now collectively known as Research4Life, making online scientific content available free or at nominal cost to researchers in developing countries. Please visit Wiley's Content Access - Corporate Citizenship site: http://www.wiley.com/WileyCDA/Section/id-390082.html

Printed in the USA by The Sheridan Group.

Address for Editorial Correspondence: Co-editors, Betsy Barefoot and Jillian L. Kinzie, New Directions for Higher Education, Email barefoot@jngi.org

Abstracting and Indexing Services
The Journal is indexed by Academic Search Alumni Edition (EBSCO Publishing); Higher Education Abstracts (Claremont Graduate University); MLA International Bibliography (MLA).

Cover design: Wiley
Cover Images: © Lava 4 images | Shutterstock

For submission instructions, subscription and all other information visit:
wileyonlinelibrary.com/journal/he

CONTENTS

EDITOR'S NOTES

The scholarship of practice stands as a nascent topic in the literature of higher education. Bringing this topic to the forefront of consideration is the primary goal of this volume of *New Directions for Higher Education*.

How then might we define the scholarship of practice? In my 2005 article in *The Review of Higher Education* titled "Reflections on a Scholarship of Practice," I stated that the two primary goals of a scholarship of practice are (1) the improvement of administrative practice in higher education, and (2) the development of a knowledge base worthy of professional status for administrative work. I add to this first goal of the improvement of administrative practice in higher education by asserting that the attainment of this particular goal entails the use of findings of empirical research as a foundation for the development of institutional policy and practice (Braxton, 2005).

Together, these assertions lead to a revised definition of the scholarship of practice as the improvement of administrative practice in higher education through the development of a knowledge base to guide such practice and the use of the findings of empirical research as a basis for the development of institutional policy and practice. This revised definition can be extended to other academic fields that serve communities of practice such as medicine, nursing, occupational therapy, and pharmacy, as well as others. This revised definition provides an organizing framework for the chapters of this volume.

The volume consists of eight chapters arrayed across three parts: Part I: The Development of Knowledge Bases for Practice; Part II: The Uses of Research Findings to Guide Practice; and Part III: Graduate Preparation and the Scholarship of Practice as Stewardship.

Part I: The Development of Knowledge Bases for Practice

This part includes two chapters that focus attention on the development of a knowledge base to guide administrative practice both in higher education and in occupational fields served by higher education. In Chapter 1, Jenna Kramer and I present our findings from a content analysis of articles published between 1996 and 2016 in *The Journal of Higher Education*, *The Review of Higher Education*, and *Research in Higher Education*. We classify the

New Directions for Higher Education, no. 178, Summer 2017 © 2017 Wiley Periodicals, Inc.
Published online in Wiley Online Library (wileyonlinelibrary.com) • DOI: 10.1002/he.20229

articles according to the forms of professional knowledge they produce and consider the implications and distribution of knowledge production over the two decades of this review. The goal of this analysis is to determine the degree to which articles published in the core journals of higher education address three types of professional knowledge delineated by Eraut (1988): replicative, applicatory, and interpretative. From our analysis, we advance conclusions about the development of a knowledge base for administrative practice in higher education.

In Chapter 2, Dawn Lyken-Segosebe examines how the scholarship of practice is being used to increase the knowledge base within hard-applied disciplines such as pharmacy and soft-applied disciplines such as nursing and occupational therapy. She also examines how the scholarship of practice is conceptualized within these disciplines and describes features that distinguish it from traditional research. Drawing from practice within these three applied disciplines, Lyken-Segosebe presents recommendations for colleges and universities regarding the implementation and recognition of the scholarship of practice for the field of higher education.

Part II: The Uses of Research Findings to Guide Practice

This part consists of three chapters that address the use of empirical research to guide the development of policy and practice as a variant of the scholarship of practice. Empirical research frequently yields findings concerning abstract concepts derived from theory. As a consequence, a conversion process is necessary to render empirically supported theoretical concepts in a form amenable to use in practice. Maureen E. Wilson and Amy S. Hirschy in Chapter 3 address this conversion process by reviewing models to translate theory into practice. In their chapter, they review process models for translating scholarship into practice and offer suggestions for choosing among those models. Administrators can apply these theories and models across disciplines. Wilson and Hirschy conclude with suggestions for interpreting and acting on research and detail implications for administrative practice.

The other two chapters of Part II provide examples of the use of the findings of empirical research to guide practice. In Chapter 4, Jillian Kinzie centers her attention on the 17-year-old assessment project known as the National Survey of Student Engagement (NSSE) to explore evidence-based practice. This chapter focuses on NSSE's emphasis on assessment to inform practice and guide institutional improvement, the crux of the scholarship of practice. Kinzie describes two categories of scholarship of practice using NSSE results—the use of results to inform and improve practice and the development of a knowledge base grounded in evidence and practitioner inquiry. In the conclusion to this chapter, Kinzie posits that administrators and faculty demonstrate their participation in the scholarship of practice by using research and assessment results as they make decisions related to institutional policy and practice.

General education provides another organizational setting for engagement in the scholarship of practice. In Chapter 5, Cynthia A. Wells asserts that general education constitutes a higher education context in which a scholarship of practice is both necessary and generative. She gives consideration to the realization of a scholarship of practice focused on general education buttressed by specific illustrations. Wells also delineates the challenges faced in such an endeavor. Thus, she presents a prototype of a scholarship of practice through specific application to general education.

Part III: Graduate Preparation and the Scholarship of Practice as Stewardship

This part includes the three remaining chapters of this volume. Chapters 6 and 7 attend to the topic of graduate preparation for engagement in the scholarship of practice. In Chapter 6, Melissa McDaniels and Erik Skogsberg call for administrators, faculty, and doctoral students to take immediate action to prepare more dynamic transdisciplinary professionals by leveraging the scholarship of practice. They discuss practices in the form of strategies that faculty and administrators can implement to compel graduate student awareness of the scholarship of practice. In Chapter 7, Amy S. Hirschy and Maureen E. Wilson highlight one professional field—college student affairs administration—as a model for inculcating the value of integrating theory and empirically based research into professional practice.

In Chapter 8, the final chapter in the volume, Todd Ream and I assert that engagement in the scholarship of practice functions as a steward for the welfare of higher education at the level of the individual college and university and at the level of higher education as a social institution. We also posit that scholars of practice and public intellectuals share some commonalities.

This volume of New Direction for Higher Education should be of interest to both the scholarly and practice communities of higher education. Members of these communities include institutional policy makers such as presidents, chief academic affairs officers, and academic deans. Members of tenure and promotion committees and scholars of higher education should also find the chapters of this volume valuable to their work. Scholarly and professional associations will also find the chapters provocative for the consideration and development of association activities.

John M. Braxton
Editor

NEW DIRECTIONS FOR HIGHER EDUCATION • DOI: 10.1002/he

References

Braxton, J. M. (2005). Reflections on a scholarship of practice. *The Review of Higher Education, 28*(2), 285–293.

Eraut, M. (1988). Knowledge creation and knowledge use in professional contexts. *Studies in Higher Education, 10,* 117–132.

JOHN M. BRAXTON *is professor of education in the Higher Education Leadership and Policy Program at Peabody College of Vanderbilt University.*

Table 1.2. Summary of Classification by Journal and Year

Year	Journal of Higher Education Volume	Population	Sample	Review of Higher Education Volume	Population	Sample	Research in Higher Education Volume	Population	Sample
1996	67	27	6	20	20	3	37	31	17
1997	68	26	12	21	23	6	38	36	21
1998	69	26	4	22	20	13	39	33	18
1999	70	38	17	23	22	11	40	36	16
2000	71	28	6	24	21	9	41	34	10
2001	72	26	6	25	21	5	42	32	16
2002	73	26	5	26	23	6	43	28	10
2003	74	27	7	27	22	14	44	31	11
2004	75	27	9	28	24	17	45	40	16
2005	76	25	8	29	18	12	46	36	14
2006	77	29	7	30	16	7	47	37	14
2007	78	24	9	31	17	10	48	33	12
2008	79	27	12	32	18	8	49	39	17
2009	80	27	6	33	17	12	50	38	21
2010	81	29	12	34	20	11	51	37	13
2011	82	32	7	35	23	12	52	40	13
2012	83	33	12	36	23	11	53	37	8
2013	84	32	7	37	17	12	54	37	11
2014	85	31	9	38	18	9	55	34	10
2015	86	30	12	39	19	11	56	36	16
2016	87	30	4	40*	5	5	57	33	11
Total		600	177		407	204		738	295
Avg		28.6	8.43		19.5	9.7		35.1	14.0

Note: Population = total articles published; Sample = scholarship of practice; *To date

articles across the three modes of knowledge. Of the articles, 278 (41% of the sample; 16% of population) produced knowledge that was replicative in nature, 252 (37% of sample; 14% of population) produced applicatory knowledge, and 146 (22% of sample; 8% of population) produced interpretative knowledge.

The average number of articles contributing to the scholarship of practice by journal varied to some degree. *The Review of Higher Education* (see Table 1.3a) averaged roughly 10 per year in a fairly tight distribution, while *The Journal of Higher Education* (see Table 1.3b) was more variable and averaged roughly eight per year. *Research in Higher Education* (see Table 1.3c) published roughly 14 articles per year in the scholarship of practice sample. There were 135 descriptive studies, mainly meta-analyses or reviews of the extant literature. Of the empirical studies ($N = 541$), 24% were qualitative. The design of most studies was cross-sectional observation, or survey. Approximately one quarter of studies were longitudinal in nature (i.e., observations gathered over more than 1 year). Randomization in the studies was much rarer: *The Review of Higher Education* and *The Journal of Higher*

Table 1.3a. Detailed Classification for *The Review of Higher Education* by Mode and Year

			The Review of Higher Education				
Year	Volume	Population	Sample	Replicative	Applicatory	Interpretative	% Classified
1996	20	20	3	2	0	1	0.150
1997	21	23	6	2	1	3	0.261
1998	22	20	13	3	7	3	0.650
1999	23	22	11	5	4	2	0.500
2000	24	21	9	4	4	1	0.429
2001	25	21	5	1	3	1	0.238
2002	26	23	6	3	3	0	0.261
2003	27	22	14	2	7	5	0.636
2004	28	24	17	4	7	6	0.708
2005	29	18	12	4	4	4	0.667
2006	30	16	7	2	1	4	0.438
2007	31	17	10	4	5	1	0.588
2008	32	18	8	2	3	3	0.444
2009	33	17	12	4	7	1	0.706
2010	34	20	11	6	3	2	0.550
2011	35	23	12	3	8	1	0.522
2012	36	23	11	6	2	3	0.478
2013	37	17	12	5	2	5	0.706
2014	38	18	9	5	1	3	0.500
2015	39	19	11	5	2	4	0.579
2016	40*	8	5	0	5	0	0.625
Total		407	204	72	79	53	
Avg		19.5	9.7	3.4	3.8	2.5	0.506

Note: Population = total articles published; Sample = scholarship of practice; *To date

Education each had two scholarship-of-practice articles in which the studies utilized some randomization; *Research in Higher Education* had 10 articles in the sample that utilized some randomization.

Much of the interpretative knowledge produced toward a higher education scholarship of practice developed as emerging issues of importance or new perspectives on important topics. For instance, in *Research in Higher Education* in the mid- to late 1990s, articles producing interpretative knowledge focused on the shift from considering college access to college retention and attainment, as well as emerging conversations about gender equity in the academy with regard to hiring, tenure, and pay. Early articles on such topics contribute to the interpretative knowledge base and pave the way for replicative and applicatory knowledge production as scholarly work comes to reflect practical and routine knowledge or technical knowledge applied to novel contexts.

Most of the articles addressed one of the previously defined topics, whereas some contended with multiple topics. Although these topics were generally spread over the 20-year period, special issues created high

New Directions for Higher Education • DOI: 10.1002/he

Table 1.3b. Detailed Classification for the *The Journal of Higher Education* by Mode and Year

Year	Volume	Population	Sample	Replicative	Applicatory	Interpretative	% Classified
			The Journal of Higher Education				
1996	67	27	6	3	1	2	0.222
1997	68	26	12	5	2	5	0.462
1998	69	26	4	2	1	1	0.154
1999	70	38	17	7	2	8	0.447
2000	71	28	6	1	0	5	0.214
2001	72	26	6	2	3	1	0.231
2002	73	26	5	2	3	0	0.192
2003	74	27	7	2	3	2	0.259
2004	75	27	9	2	5	2	0.333
2005	76	25	8	4	2	2	0.320
2006	77	29	7	2	4	1	0.241
2007	78	24	9	3	5	1	0.375
2008	79	27	12	0	7	5	0.444
2009	80	27	6	1	4	1	0.222
2010	81	29	12	3	8	1	0.414
2011	82	32	7	3	2	2	0.219
2012	83	33	12	3	3	6	0.364
2013	84	32	7	0	4	3	0.219
2014	85	31	9	3	5	1	0.290
2015	86	30	12	3	3	6	0.400
2016	87	30	4	2	2	0	0.133
Total		600	177	53	69	55	
Yearly avg		28.6	8.4	2.5	3.3	2.6	0.293

Note: Population = total articles published; Sample = scholarship of practice

density on areas of contemporary importance during the period of review. With regard to faculty, most articles were related to tenure, either in structures surrounding the review process or the trend toward more contingent faculty. These articles were classified as contributing to either applicatory or interpretative forms of professional knowledge.

The student-experience articles largely focused on postsecondary transition, supports, and outcomes for students by race, first-generation status, and gender. Many of the student-centered articles focused on extracurricular institutional programming and supports and research-mentoring by faculty. These student-centered articles were classified as either contributing to replicative or applicatory forms of professional knowledge.

In the realm of administration, the research largely fell into three areas: leadership in practice, institutional structures, and finances. Organizational structure among staff and faculty was a frequent topic of study during this period. These administratively focused articles were mostly classified as contributing to applicatory forms of professional knowledge.

Table 1.3c. Detailed Classification for *Research in Higher Education* by Mode and Year

				Research in Higher Education			
Year	Volume	Population	Sample	Replicative	Applicatory	Interpretative	% Classified
1996	37	31	17	10	5	2	0.548
1997	38	36	21	6	11	4	0.583
1998	39	33	18	7	5	6	0.545
1999	40	36	16	9	6	1	0.444
2000	41	34	10	2	7	1	0.294
2001	42	32	16	3	9	4	0.500
2002	43	28	10	4	5	1	0.357
2003	44	31	11	6	5	0	0.355
2004	45	40	16	6	7	3	0.400
2005	46	36	14	6	7	1	0.389
2006	47	37	14	6	5	3	0.378
2007	48	33	12	10	2	0	0.364
2008	49	39	17	12	4	1	0.436
2009	50	38	21	13	5	3	0.553
2010	51	37	13	7	4	2	0.351
2011	52	40	13	7	5	1	0.325
2012	53	37	8	5	1	2	0.216
2013	54	37	11	9	1	1	0.297
2014	55	34	10	7	2	1	0.294
2015	56	36	16	9	6	1	0.444
2016	57	33	11	9	2	0	0.333
Total		738	295	153	104	38	
Avg		35.1	14.0	7.3	5.0	1.8	0.400

Note: Population = total articles published; Sample = scholarship of practice

Nevertheless, some of these articles were viewed as interpretative professional knowledge.

Curriculum articles, which were largely classified as applicatory and to some extent interpretative, contended with faculty perceptions of and adoption to trends in undergraduate teaching and learning during this period: service-learning, technology, and undergraduate research.

We found there to be greater evidence of a scholarship of practice than we anticipated. Much of the knowledge generated by studies holds utility for administrators of varying capacities and seniority. Although the bulk of the replicative and applicatory knowledge generated was important in its ability to describe the current characteristics and challenges of the contemporary college student, it appeared, however, to be less useful as a roadmap for successful practice. Perhaps this perception of limited utility derives from the difficulty of crystallizing deep professional knowledge into article-length pieces; perhaps these ends are better achieved through volumes and books.

NEW DIRECTIONS FOR HIGHER EDUCATION • DOI: 10.1002/he

2

This chapter examines how the scholarship of practice is being used within applied disciplines and offers recommendations for colleges and universities regarding the implementation of the scholarship of practice for the discipline of higher education.

The Scholarship of Practice in Applied Disciplines

Dawn Lyken-Segosebe

Over 25 years have passed since Boyer (1990) published his book *Scholarship Reconsidered: Priorities of the Professoriate*. The impact of this influential text on the disciplines is evident in how scholarship is being applied to improve disciplinary practice. It is evident in the development of a "scholarship of practice," which seeks to bridge the gap between the theories developed and research findings obtained by academicians and the questions asked and approaches adopted by practitioners in their daily work. Practitioners assert that theory and research are often irrelevant to their everyday work and difficult to implement due to the tendency for academicians to emphasize scientific rigor over relevance (Kielhofner, 2005a). According to Schon (1987),

> In recent years, there has been a growing perception that researchers, who are supposed to feed the professional schools with useful knowledge, have less and less to say that practitioners find useful .... Martin Rein and Sheldon White (1980) have recently observed that research not only is separate from professional practice but has been increasingly captured by its own agenda, divergent from the needs of professional practitioners. (p. 10)

The scholarship of practice addresses this concern about the relevance and utility for practice (e.g., ease, efficiency, and effectiveness of professional communication) and graduate education of the theories developed and research findings obtained by academicians (Kielhofner, 2005b). By coupling knowledge generation and knowledge use "into a single enterprise," the scholarship of practice recognizes that there is knowledge in practice in addition to knowledge for practice (Kielhofner, 2005b; Usher & Bryant, 1987).

NEW DIRECTIONS FOR HIGHER EDUCATION, no. 178, Summer 2017 © 2017 Wiley Periodicals, Inc.
Published online in Wiley Online Library (wileyonlinelibrary.com) • DOI: 10.1002/he.20231

Pursuit of the scholarship of practice has improved practice in both soft- and hard-applied disciplines. Storer (1967, 1972) and Biglan (1973a, 1973b) characterized academic disciplines as having pure-applied as well as hard-soft dimensions. Soft disciplines (e.g., nursing, occupational therapy, business, and accounting) have lower levels of paradigmatic development. Practitioners in these disciplines exhibit less agreement regarding appropriate research questions for their field and appropriate methodologies for addressing these questions. Hard disciplines (e.g., pharmacy, engineering, and agriculture) have high paradigmatic development. There are high levels of agreement among practitioners regarding issues such as appropriate research topics and methods (Braxton & Hargens, 1996).

This chapter examines how the scholarship of practice is being used to increase the knowledge base within the soft-applied disciplines of nursing and occupational therapy and the hard-applied discipline of pharmacy. It examines how the scholarship of practice is conceptualized within these disciplines and the features that distinguish it from traditional research. Drawing from practice within these three applied disciplines, recommendations are presented for colleges and universities regarding the implementation and recognition of the scholarship of practice for the discipline of higher education.

The Scholarship of Practice in Soft-Applied Disciplines—Nursing and Occupational Therapy

Within the soft-applied disciplines of nursing and occupational therapy, the scholarship of practice is comparable to Boyer's (1990) scholarship of application. These two types of scholarship are considered similar given that Boyer's scholarship of application "emphasizes the use of new knowledge in solving society's problems and corresponds closely to later descriptions of the scholarship of practice" (Jones & Van Ort, 2001, p. 141). Specifically, Boyer asserts that in conducting scholarship application, the scholar addresses the questions: "How can knowledge be responsibly applied to consequential problems? How can it be helpful to individuals as well as institutions?" And further, "Can social problems themselves define an agenda for scholarly investigation?" (p. 21).

The Scholarship of Practice in Nursing. The American Nurses Association defines nursing as "the protection, promotion, and optimization of health and abilities, prevention of illness and injury, facilitation of healing, alleviation of suffering through the diagnosis and treatment of human response, and advocacy in the care of individuals, families, groups, communities, and populations" (http://www.nursingworld.org/).

Nursing presents a special case for an examination of the scholarship of practice because it represents an academic discipline that has professional mandates. Nurse academicians may function as advanced practice nurses (APNs) who perform clinical practice activities. In addition to their more vigorous partner in the search for answers to our most pressing social, civic, economic, and moral problems" (p. 18). The scholarships of application and engagement overlap in a scholarship of practice when the research addresses societal problems. Smith et al. (2005) provide examples of engaged pharmacy scholarship that constitute the scholarship of practice. They include research undertaken by Ohio State University's faculty, postdoctoral fellows and residents, and students to "... discover, disseminate and apply knowledge to enhance public health" and "develop and implement pharmacy practices to improve medication access, effectiveness, and safety for patients" (Smith et al., 2005, p. 3). Another example is the University of Mississippi School of Pharmacy's 2001 collaboration with the Aaron E. Henry Community Health Center (CHC) in Clarksdale, Mississippi on the "Effective Pharmaceutical Care in the Mississippi Delta: a Demonstration Project" through a two-year federal grant from the Health Resources and Services Administration.

The collaboration sought to improve primary care services for uninsured and underserved citizens in the Mississippi Delta, demonstrate an innovative method of providing clinical pharmacy services to asthma and diabetes patients served by the community health center, and help the community health center expand access to low-cost drugs and care for its patients (Smith et al., 2005). The collaboration included University of Mississippi's School of Pharmacy faculty, retail pharmacists, and CHC's staff physicians. Data were collected and analyses performed to document the outcomes associated with the intervention. Early findings, specifically with asthma, indicated significant impact of the intervention on the frequency of occurrence of acute attacks and the resultant hospitalization costs (American Association of Colleges of Pharmacy, 2003).

Implications for the Scholarship of Practice in Higher Education

This chapter investigates the scholarship of practice in the soft-applied disciplines of nursing and occupational therapy and the hard-applied discipline of pharmacy. Within the disciplines of nursing and occupational therapy, the scholarship of practice is comparable to Boyer's (1990) scholarship of application. Within the discipline of pharmacy, it occurs as Boyer's scholarship of application and Boyer's (1996) scholarship of engagement. It is important that the presence in the three applied disciplines of the scholarship of practice in the form of application scholarship not be considered indicative of what the scholarship of practice generally looks like in all applied disciplines. The three disciplines have clinical elements and distinguish between academic and clinical faculty—distinctions that may not be present in other applied disciplines. Other forms of Boyer's scholarship may characterize the scholarship of practice in other applied disciplines.

NEW DIRECTIONS FOR HIGHER EDUCATION • DOI: 10.1002/he

How the scholarship of practice is conceptualized and what it looks like in the applied disciplines of nursing, occupational therapy, and pharmacy present learning points for the discipline of higher education. At least four recommendations can be made for colleges and universities regarding a scholarship of practice in the higher education discipline:

1. Higher education institutions must recognize the value afforded by a scholarship of practice in the higher education discipline.

The scholarship of practice in nursing, occupational therapy, and pharmacy is oriented around client/patient outcomes and health care. The scholarship utilizes knowledge of practice to generate knowledge for practice. The knowledge generated is valued because it enhances practice and practice outcomes and enables a better understanding of clients/patients and their needs. Like nursing, occupational therapy, and pharmacy, the higher education discipline is also a client-centered practice; it is oriented around the college and university student and his/her outcomes. As in the applied disciplines, the scholarship of practice affords improved practice toward the student-client and improved student outcomes. Colleges and universities should recognize and value these functions of the scholarship of practice. They should recognize that a scholarship of practice in the higher education discipline has the capacity to improve student outcomes, and administrative and institutional practice by applying knowledge of higher education to assess various student outcomes, develop innovative student engagement and success strategies, illuminate and evaluate the effectiveness of specific student services, analyze student services/teaching and learning delivery models, and develop and assess administrative practices, institutional policy, and state/national higher education policy.

The client or student is not the sole potential beneficiary. The university, the community, the discipline, and its faculty also benefit from the scholarship of practice. Higher education institutions should also consider that when the scholarship of practice takes the forms of application and engaged scholarship, it benefits the institution itself by enabling it to meet its service obligation and "provides evidence for financial support by allowing a broad range of constituencies (e.g., citizens, organizations) to understand how the academic organization makes contributions to enhance the quality of their lives" (Popovich & Abel, 2002, p. 61).

2. Higher education institutions must widen the definition and direction of scholarship.

In conjunction with valuing the potential contributions of a scholarship of higher education practice, colleges and universities must formally recognize it as a valid form of scholarship. In particular, the existing conception of scholarship requires redefinition in higher education institutions. The gap between theory and research on one hand and practice on the other is related to the too narrow definition of scholarship within the academic community. Scholarship tends to be defined in terms of basic or theoretical research published in peer-reviewed journals (Boyer, 1990; O'Meara,

2006). Furthermore, such theoretical research is often considered as the precursor to practice with practice flowing from theory in a linear, unidirectional manner. In his investigation of nursing scholarship, Kielhofner (2005b) notes that researchers have traditionally expected knowledge created to guide practice. He states, " . . . we have bestowed upon our theory and research the authority to specify what should go on in practice while mostly leaving the problem of how to actualize those specifications to the practitioner" (Kielhofner, 2005b, p. 232).

Boyer (1990) also recognizes both the narrowness of the definition of scholarship, and the perceived linearity and unidirectional nature of the relationship between scholarship and practice. He states that

> what we have now is a more restricted view of scholarship, one that limits it to a hierarchy of functions. Basic research has come to be viewed as the first and most essential form of scholarly activity, with other functions flowing from it. Scholars are academics who conduct research, publish, and then perhaps convey their knowledge to students or apply what they have learned. The latter functions grow out of scholarship, they are not considered a part of it. But knowledge is not necessarily developed in such a linear manner. (p. 15)

Higher education institutions need to formally widen their definition of scholarship to include the scholarship of practice and recognize that theory and practice may flow to and from each other in a multi-directional relationship. According to Burgener (2001),

> The recognition and acceptance of the potential contributions of a broadened definition of scholarship, encompassing experiential ways of knowing, may assist in closing the existing gap between what is recognized and valued as scholarship in academic settings and the continuing unmet needs of the larger society. (p. 48)

3. Higher education institutions must review the traditional triad reward system of teaching, scholarship, and service to include professional practice and recognize practice as a form of scholarship in the promotion and tenure process for specified disciplines such as the discipline of higher education.

A broader definition of scholarship must necessarily be accompanied by the accommodation of practice within institutional reward systems. Three proposals may be offered in this regard. First, it may be proposed that higher education institutions draw from the American Association of Colleges of Nursing's (AACN, 1999) definition of scholarship as activities that advance the teaching, research, and practice of the discipline. Practice should formally be considered across the board as part of the institutional reward system. However, the reward system should also reflect that practice is not relevant to or expected of all disciplines. Second, it may be proposed that what specifically constitutes the scholarship of practice should be discipline-determined. Essentially, a higher education department would determine which activities constitute the scholarship of practice for its faculty members. Diamond (2002) proposes that individual academic disciplines can be given the responsibility of determining if a specific activity meets the criteria for achieving scholarship goals identified by the department. He argues that this approach would enable promotion and tenure review committees to focus their attention on the quality of the portfolio and process rather than on whether the activity should be considered scholarly.

With department-determined scholarly activities in place, promotion and tenure review committees can then apply a consistent approach across all practice disciplines toward the review of material presented as evidence of the scholarship of practice. Finkelstein's (2001) proposal for a unified view of scholarship for faculty involved in community engagement is relevant here. Third, and drawing from the central tenets of Finkelstein's proposal, it may be proposed that promotion and tenure review committees in higher education institutions adopt a consistent definition and assessment of, and documentation for, the scholarship of practice. Promotion and tenure committees may define the scholarship of practice in higher education in terms of the six characteristics of scholarly work that Diamond and Adam (1995, 2000) identify in their publication, *The Disciplines Speak: Rewarding the Scholarly, Professional, and Creative Work of Faculty*. Scholarly work should therefore be accepted as scholarship of practice if:

1. The activity requires a high level of discipline-related expertise.
2. The activity breaks new ground, is innovative.
3. The activity can be replicated or elaborated.
4. The work and its results can be documented.
5. The work and its results can be peer-reviewed.
6. The activity has significance or impact.

These characteristics are consistent with the American Association of Colleges of Nursing's (1999) identification of scholarly work as activity embracing rigorous inquiry that is significant to the profession, creative, can be documented, can be replicated or elaborated, and can be peer-reviewed through various methods.

Promotion and tenure review committees may assess scholarly activity for practice in higher education using the assessment standards identified in Glassick, Huber, and Maeroff's (1997) *Scholarship Assessed*. Drawing on the findings of a 1994 survey on changes in policies and procedures with regard to faculty evaluation conducted at all four-year colleges and universities in the United States, Glassick et al. proposed six standards for assessing scholarship that would work across all domains of faculty scholarship— namely the extent to which faculty members establish clear goals, are adequately prepared, use appropriate methods, have significant results, effectively present their work, and perform a reflective critique of their work (Finkelstein, 2001).

4. Higher education institutions must recognize the collaborative nature of the scholarship of practice in the higher education discipline. The review of scholarship in the disciplines of nursing, occupational therapy, and pharmacy reveals that the scholarship of practice especially in the form of the scholarship of application has the capacity to be collaborative. In the higher-education discipline, such collaboration may involve tenured and tenure-track faculty, professors of the practice, administrators in colleges and universities, graduate students in higher education as a field of study, institutional research officers, researchers working in think tanks, statewide coordinating boards, and national higher education organizations such as the Institute of Higher Education Policy, the American Council on Education, and the Association of American Colleges and Universities (Braxton, 2005).

Higher education institutions should recognize that such partnerships give rise to scholarly work that improves practice, and that "nontraditional" researchers or practitioners can contribute to the knowledge-generation process. Colleges and universities should appreciate the time commitments required to establish such partnerships and conduct research for practice.

Closing Thoughts

In closing, a scholarship of practice seeks to bridge the gap between the theories developed and research findings obtained by academicians and the questions asked and approaches adopted by practitioners in their daily work. It overcomes problems related to the irrelevance and lack of utility of theories and research to practice. The pursuit of the scholarship of practice has improved the knowledge base and practice in the soft-applied disciplines of nursing and occupational therapy and the hard-applied discipline of pharmacy.

The higher education discipline can learn from the ways such scholarship is conceptualized and implemented in these applied fields. However, a recurring factor regarding the implementation and recognition of the scholarship of practice in the higher education discipline remains the need for colleges and universities to promote and implement faculty reward systems that recognize and give weight to forms of scholarship beyond the traditional form of discovery scholarship.

References

American Association of Colleges of Nursing. (1999). *Position statement on defining scholarship for the discipline of nursing*. Retrieved from http://www.aacn.nche.edu/publications/position/defining-scholarship

American Association of Colleges of Pharmacy, Commission to Implement Change in Pharmaceutical Education. (1993). *What is the mission of pharmaceutical education?* Background Paper 1. Retrieved from http://www.aacp.org/resources/historicaldocuments/Documents/BackgroundPaper1.pdf

American Association of Colleges of Pharmacy. (2003). *Successful practices in pharmaceutical Education, 2002: Academia-practice interface.* Retrieved from http://www.aacp.org/resources/education/Documents/2002Academia-Practice.pdf

The American Occupational Therapy Association. (2016). *The American Occupational Therapy Association.* Retrieved from www.aota.org

Biglan, A. (1973a). The characteristics of subject matter in different academic areas. *Journal of Applied Psychology, 57*(3), 195–203.

Biglan, A. (1973b). Relationships between subject matter characteristics and the structure and output of university departments. *Journal of Applied Psychology, 57*(3), 204–213.

Bonsaksen, T., Celo, C., Myraunet, I., Granå, K., & Ellingham, B. (2005). Promoting academic-practice partnerships through students' practice placement. In P. Crist & G. A. Kielhofner (Eds.), *The scholarship of practice: Academic-practice collaborations for promoting occupational therapy.* New York, NY: Haworth Press.

Boyer E. L. (1990). *Scholarship reconsidered: Priorities for the professoriate.* Princeton, NJ: The Carnegie Foundation for the Advancement of Teaching.

Boyer, E. L. (1996). The scholarship of engagement. *Bulletin of the American Academy of Arts and Sciences, 49*(7), 18–33.

Braxton, J. M. (2005). Reflections on a scholarship of practice. *The Review of Higher Education, 28*(2), 285–293.

Braxton, J. M., & Hargens, L. (1996). Variation among academic disciplines: Analytical frameworks and research. In J. Smart (Ed.), *Higher education: Handbook of Research and Theory,* Vol. 11 (pp. 1–46). New York, NY: Agathon Press.

Burgener S. C. (2001). Scholarship of practice for a practice profession. *Journal of Professional Nursing, 17*(1), 46–54.

Diamond, R. M. (2002). Defining scholarship for the twenty-first century. In K. Zahorski (Ed.), *New directions for teaching and learning: No. 90, Scholarship in the postmodern era: New venues, new values, new visions* (pp. 73–79). San Francisco, CA: Jossey-Bass.

Diamond, R. M., & Adam, B. E. (1995). *The disciplines speak: Rewarding the scholarly, professional, and creative work of faculty.* Washington, DC: American Association for Higher Education.

Diamond, R. M., & Adam, B. E. (2000). *The disciplines speak II: Rewarding the scholarly, professional, and creative work of faculty.* Washington, DC: American Association for Higher Education.

Finkelstein, M. A. (2001). Toward a unified view of scholarship: Eliminating tensions between traditional and engaged work. *Journal of Higher Education Outreach and Engagement, 6*(2), 35–44.

Glassick, C. E., Huber, M. T., & Maeroff, G. I. (1997). *Scholarship assessed: Evaluation of the professoriate.* San Francisco, CA: Jossey-Bass.

Holland, B. A. (2005). *Scholarship and mission in the 21st century: The role of engagement.* Paper and PowerPoint presentation for keynote address to the Australian Universities Quality Agency Forum. Retrieved from http://www.auqa.edu.au/auqf/2005/program/day1.html

Jones, E. G., & Van Ort, S. (2001). Facilitating scholarship among clinical faculty. *Journal of Professional Nursing, 17*(3), 141–146.

Kennedy, R. H., Gubbins, P. O., Luer, M., Reddy, I. K., & Light, K. E. (2003). Developing and sustaining a culture of scholarship. *American Journal of Pharmaceutical Education, 67*(3), 1–18.

Kielhofner, G. A. (2001). *A scholarship of practice*. Paper presented at the American Occupational Therapy Association Conference.

Kielhofner, G. A. (2005a). A scholarship of practice: Creating discourse between theory, research and practice. In P. Crist & G. A. Kielhofner (Eds.), *The scholarship of practice: Academic-practice collaborations for promoting occupational therapy* (pp. 7–16). New York, NY: Haworth Press.

Kielhofner, G. A. (2005b). Research concepts in clinical scholarship—Scholarship and practice: Bridging the divide. *American Journal of Occupational Therapy, 59*(2) 231–239.

Leslie, S. W., Corcoran, G. B., MacKichan, J. J., Undie, A. S., Vanderveen, R. P., & Miller, K. W. (2004). Pharmacy scholarship reconsidered: The Report of the 2003–2004 Research and Graduate Affairs Committee. *American Journal of Pharmaceutical Education, 68*(4), 1–5.

O'Meara, K. (2006). Encouraging multiple forms of scholarship in faculty reward systems: Influence on faculty work life. *Planning for Higher Education, 34,* 43–53.

Peterson, K., & Stevens, J. (2013). Integrating the scholarship of practice into the nurse academician portfolio. *Nursing Faculty Publications*. Paper 1. Retrieved from http://digitalcommons.brockport.edu/nursing_facpub/1

Popovich, N. G., & Abel, S. R. (2002). The need for a broadened definition of faculty scholarship and creativity. *American Journal of Pharmaceutical Education, 66*(1), 59–65.

Riley, J. M., Beal, J., Levi, P., & McCausland, M. P. (2002). Revisioning nursing scholarship. *Journal of Nursing Scholarship, 34*(4), 383–389.

Schon, D. A. (1987). *Educating the reflective practitioner: Toward a new design for teaching and learning in the professions*. San Francisco, CA: Jossey-Bass.

Smith, R. E., Kerr, R. A., Nahata, M. C., Roche, V. F., Wells, B. G., & Maine, L. L. (2005). Engaging communities: Academic pharmacy addressing unmet public health needs: Report of the 2004–05 Argus Commission. *American Journal of Pharmaceutical Education, 69*(5), 1–10.

Storer, N. W. (1967). The hard sciences and the soft: some sociological observations. *Bulletin of the American Medical Association, 55*(1), 75–84.

Storer, N. W. (1972). Relations among scientific disciplines. In S. Z. Nagi & R. G. Corwin (Eds.), *The social contexts of research* (pp. 229–268). New York, NY: Wiley.

Stringer, E. T. (1996). *Action research: A handbook for practitioners*. Thousand Oaks, CA: Sage.

Taylor, R. R., Fisher, G., & Kielhofner, G. (2005). Synthesizing research, education, and practice according to the Scholarship of Practice Model: Two faculty examples. In P. Crist & G. A. Kielhofner (Eds.), *The scholarship of practice: Academic-practice collaborations for promoting occupational therapy* (pp. 107–122). New York, NY: Haworth Press.

Usher, R., & Bryant, I. (1987). Re-examining the theory-practice relationship in continuing professional education. *Studies in Higher Education, 12*(2), 201–212.

DAWN LYKEN-SEGOSEBE *is a lecturer at the Botswana International University of Science and Technology. Her research focuses on the scholarly and teaching role performance of college and university faculty, colleges and universities as organizations, the college student experience, STEM education, and the internationalization of higher education.*

Models for applying scholarship to practice provide guidance to administrators who are informed by research to address very complex problems.

3

Models for Applying Scholarship to Practice

Maureen E. Wilson, Amy S. Hirschy

A goal of the scholarship of practice is to improve professional practice by using empirical research as the groundwork for developing practice and policy (Braxton, 2014). Research should contribute to an understanding of the challenges practitioners face. The purpose of this chapter is to review process models for translating scholarship into practice and offer suggestions for choosing among those models. Administrators can apply these theories and models across disciplines. We conclude with suggestions for interpreting and acting on research and detail implications for administrative practice.

Model of Theory-to-Practice Translation

Reason and Kimball (2012, 2013) reviewed and critiqued theory-to-practice models and then presented a new model for integrating scholarship, context, and reflection. As pictured in Figure 3.1, the model incorporates formal theory, institutional context, informal theory, and practice as well as feedback loops from practice to informal theory, institutional context, and formal theory. These feedback loops are a key contribution of Reason and Kimball's (2013) model compared to existing models and guiding principles (e.g., Bensimon, 2007; Rodgers & Widick, 1980; Stage & Dannells, 2000). Although Reason and Kimball grounded their analysis in student affairs, the model can apply more broadly to higher education administration as well.

Formal Theory. Reason and Kimball (2012) argued persuasively that practitioners "must have a broad-based, advanced education in [formal] theories that allows for an informed, eclectic approach to theory selection at all administrative levels" (p. 368). Formal theories offer shared language and understanding among professionals. At the formal theory stage of the model, practitioners should identify which theories are known by

NEW DIRECTIONS FOR HIGHER EDUCATION, no. 178, Summer 2017 © 2017 Wiley Periodicals, Inc.
Published online in Wiley Online Library (wileyonlinelibrary.com) • DOI: 10.1002/he.20232

Figure 3.1. Theory-to-practice translation model (Reason & Kimball, 2013)

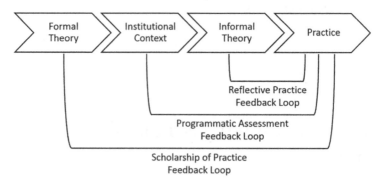

staff members, what new perspectives have been offered via publications and conference presentations, the outcomes proposed in the theories, and the populations included in and excluded from the research that led to the theories (Reason & Kimball, 2012).

Institutional Context. Examining institutional context or culture happens at the second stage of the model. Reason and Kimball (2012) credited the case-study approach of Stage (1994) and Stage and Dannells (2000) as possibly being the only theory-to-practice models in student affairs that explicitly integrated institutional culture into the process. More than just institutional type, size, and selectivity, culture, or context includes the community members' values, beliefs, and perceptions. In Reason and Kimball's (2013) model, institutional context is intended to capture the ways in which the environment affects institutionally supported goals and how best to accomplish them. Implicitly and explicitly, practitioners' knowledge and use of their informal theories are influenced by the institutional context. Adapting Reason and Kimball's (2012) recommended questions for student affairs practitioners in this stage of the model, we suggest the following questions for other higher education professionals:

1. What are the sociodemographic characteristics of students and faculty and staff members at the institution?
2. Who influences the goals for the institution and how do the culture of the institution and the composition of the administration, faculty, staff, and students influence those goals?
3. What educational values and beliefs do faculty and staff members hold?
4. How do these values and beliefs shape interactions between and among community members?

Considering these questions about a particular institution may help higher education administrators tailor their approaches to addressing specific community issues.

Informal Theory. The third stage of Reason and Kimball's (2013) model focuses on informal theory which is "common knowledge that allows us to make implicit connections among the events and persons in our environment and upon which we act in everyday life" (Parker, 1977, p. 421). Reason and Kimball (2012) contended that informal theories are based upon the convergence of formal theories, institutional context, and the positionality of individual professionals. Positionality reflects an understanding and acknowledgment of the influences of one's experiences and social identities on one's assumptions and beliefs (Jones, Torres, & Arminio, 2014). In other words, professionals' positionality shapes their informal theories. Key to Reason and Kimball's (2012) contention is that formal theories explicitly shape informal theories and this connection is critical to professional practice. They noted Parker's (1977) suggestion that practitioners may not be aware of their informal theories and that Bensimon (2007) did not clearly address the link between formal and implicit or informal theories. Reason and Kimball (2012) argued that "informal theory implies a desirable level of critical consciousness and reflection that implicit theory does not" (p. 360). Furthermore, we add that the majority of college and university administrators are trained in their academic discipline instead of administration, and thus many are likely unfamiliar with existing theoretical models in higher education administration. Additionally, their experience may span multiple institutions, and some may fail to uncover and appreciate institutional context as a critical factor in decision-making, assuming that what worked in a prior setting is easily transferable to the current institution. They may rely on informal theories not well anchored to formal theories or even institutional context.

At the informal theory stage of the model, Reason and Kimball (2012) encouraged professionals to consider questions pertaining to their beliefs about how learning and development occur, how their informal theories are influenced by their educational experiences and institutional context, and how their understanding of formal theory affects their understanding of learning and development. We also advise that administrators consider the influences of their positionality on their informal theories. Again, student affairs professionals may frame these questions in terms of student learning and development. Depending on the task or focus, other campus professionals may also focus on student learning and development, perhaps having never studied formal theories related to those processes. However, their focus may also involve other aspects and populations of the campus community. For example, how can institutional leaders build and strengthen the pipeline for campus leadership roles (e.g., academic department chairs, college deans, administrative directors)? In that context, they may think about what draws faculty and staff to seek or accept leadership roles on campus. Their own journeys to leadership roles, observations of others who ascended to those positions, and their views of institutional efforts to recruit campus leaders may shape their informal theories. They may also draw upon formal theories of andragogy, administration, and leadership.

Practice. In the next stage of the model, practice is the application of informal theory—informed by institutional context and formal theory—to professionals' work (Reason & Kimball, 2012). For student affairs professionals, this may be work with individual students and student groups. For the provost, this may be work with individual colleges and all academic administrators (e.g., deans and department chairs). Again adapting Reason and Kimball's guiding questions, professionals might ask themselves what work experiences have been effective or ineffective in producing intended outcomes.

Reflective Practice Feedback Loop. The first feedback loop in the model is from practice to informal theory. Reason and Kimball (2012) promoted reflective practice in which each interaction is an occasion to learn and better understand the informal theories that inform practice. They stated that "Practitioners' reactions, informal and formal assessments, and student feedback reinforce or change practitioners' understanding of the informal theories with which they work" (p. 370). Practice transforms based on changes in one's informal theories. Questions at this stage encourage professionals to consider which interventions they commonly utilize, the connections between those interventions and their informal theories, and evidence on the effectiveness of those interventions.

Programmatic Assessment Feedback Loop. The second feedback loop from practice to institutional context is critical to good assessment activities. Here the focus is on whether programs and interventions are meeting their stated goals and are still appropriate to the institutional context. Therefore, administrators should seek evidence on program effectiveness and examine how that evidence supports or refutes shared values, beliefs, and perceptions about important goals (Reason & Kimball, 2012).

Scholarship of Practice Feedback Loop. The third feedback loop from practice to formal theory enhances the process of integrating practice with scholarship and scholarship with practice. This loop helps to make practitioners visible in the development and revision of formal theory and should aid scholars in strengthening the implications of their work for practice. Similar to important questions in the reflective practice loop, professionals should consider the linkages between their interventions and formal theories and examine the evidence regarding the effectiveness of those programs, services, and policies.

Action Inquiry Model

As Reason and Kimball (2012) noted, not all practice models explicitly address the role of theory in practice. St. John, McKinney, and Tuttle's (2006)

Action Inquiry Model is one such framework. Although it does not explicitly address the role of theory, it does draw on scholarship to improve practice. St. John et al. discussed various approaches to change in higher education and argued that omitting evaluation from the change process hampers learning and adaptation. There are many persistent problems in postsecondary education, and their roots are not obvious. Therefore, instead of forging ahead uncritically with strategies that are ill suited for the problem, professionals must first develop a clear and complex understanding of myriad contributors to the problem under consideration. This is especially important in higher education, they contended, because most research focuses on traditional institutions and traditional-aged students but vexing challenges often pertain to nontraditional students, settings, and institutions. St. John et al. presented the Action Inquiry Model that consists of five complex steps.

1. **Build an understanding of the challenge.** Before proceeding to solutions, administrators must know why the challenge exists, the efficacy of past attempts to address it, and aspects of the challenge that have been inadequately addressed and those that require additional study. To understand the challenge, administrators generate potential explanations for the challenge they face and determine whether the data support the explanations. Again, they may utilize theory to help generate testable hypotheses. We propose that both formal and informal theories can help administrators build an understanding of the challenge.
2. **Look internally and externally for solutions.** Internally, administrators should have discussions on campus to understand how professionals have addressed related problems. Externally, "best practices" related to the challenge should be considered to determine whether they can be adapted to fit specific campus needs. By visiting other campuses with similar challenges, administrators can learn what approaches have been tried elsewhere and consider their suitability to the current context.
3. **Assess possible solutions.** Based on the understanding of the problem, professionals should generate options and determine whether they will address the challenge. They must identify the potential for pilot testing, benchmarks for success, and data required to determine their effectiveness.
4. **Develop action plans.** Professionals should develop action plans to implement solutions and pilot test them. It is often best to begin with plans that can be implemented with current staff and resources because seeking additional funding can impede the change process.
5. **Implement pilot test and evaluate.** Finally, the chosen solution should be pilot tested and evaluated. Administrators should use the

results of the evaluation to improve the strategy and seek support for additional resources if necessary.

Selecting Theoretically Derived Models

The Model of Theory-to-Practice Translation (Reason & Kimball, 2012) and the Action Inquiry Model (St. John et al., 2006) are just two of myriad models available to guide the application of scholarship to practice. Hirschy (2015) described many deterrents administrators face in using theoretically derived models in practice including questionable relevance, insufficient detail, uneven quality, and lack of time and training. However, use of empirically based models can aid administrators in identifying how institutional levers (e.g., resources, policies, programs) can be effectively used to achieve stated goals. She offered recommendations for selecting theoretically derived models to improve outcomes based on four criteria.

1. **Professional judgment.** Theory, practice, research and scholarship, collegial discussions, and professional engagement collectively inform professional judgment to enhance administrative practice (Blimling, 2011). Thus, administrators should use professional judgment to assess the fit of models and theories to design effective practice. Through this process, they should note which models (in whole or part) resonate with the institutional context (e.g., student characteristics, community values) and offer the greatest potential to shape strategic actions (Hirschy, 2015).
2. **Level and context of model.** Robert Merton (1968) referred to a theory as "a set of logically interrelated assumptions from which empirically testable hypotheses are derived" (p. 66). Scholars classify theories to differentiate among their characteristics, such as scope. For example, grand theories provide the broadest explanation of phenomenon, applicable in all contexts. Grand theories explain large-scale topics applicable to all types of organizations (e.g., Astin's 1984 theory of student involvement). Middle-range theories are less expansive than grand theories (e.g., Bean and Metzner's 1985 conceptual model for nontraditional students) but are applicable to multiple settings and similar groups (e.g., residential colleges or low-income students). Low-level theories explain behaviors in specific settings (e.g., Comeaux and Harrison's 2011 model for Division I student athlete success). Middle-range and low-level theories are most relevant to practitioners as they are most sensitive to contexts (Hirschy, 2015). In selecting theories, Hirschy (2015) urged practitioners to know the institution and its characteristics well in order to assess effectively the applicability of theoretical models. To do so, professionals must maintain relationships with institutional research staff to access necessary data. Administrators should carefully weigh the strengths and

weaknesses of grand, middle-range, and low-level models based on the problems they are addressing. Finally, they should consider the models most relevant to the available data. For example, leaders in strategic enrollment management should employ models that examine key enrollment indicators (i.e., student and institutional attributes).

3. **Theoretical lens and empirical support.** To determine the usefulness of a theory or model, administrators must understand the details of its development. For example, from what population was it developed? Is it generalizable to the current context? Is there empirical support for it? To make these determinations, they must read widely and choose carefully, examining the institutional challenges faced through multiple theoretical lenses.

4. **Flexibility in applying a model or models to practice.** Based on the specific challenges administrators are facing, they should weigh the advantages and disadvantages of using a single model versus drawing upon several models to best shape their practice, while considering institutional goals and characteristics. "Drawing on multiple disciplinary lenses may offer a more complex analysis and help create innovative interventions for improved practice" (Hirschy, 2015, p. 280). Patton, Renn, Guido, and Quaye (2016) concurred with this approach, arguing that examining situations through multiple theoretical lenses offers a more comprehensive understanding of the issues at hand and helps generate a variety of strategies to address them.

Interpreting and Acting on Research to Improve Administrative Practice

At the beginning of the chapter, we noted that a goal of the scholarship of practice is to improve professional practice by using empirical research as the groundwork for developing practice and policy. In addition to collecting and analyzing data generated from one's own campus to understand and address identified problems, published scholarship can aid administrators in developing a broader and more complex understanding of the issues they face.

Mayhew et al. (2016) also offered two pieces of sage guidance on interpreting and acting upon research to inform administrative practice. First, although empirical research may reveal statistically significant findings, those differences may not be practically significant. Therefore, administrators must critically examine research results to determine their relevance to local problems. We add that if they lack the expertise to understand and interpret the findings, they must bring to the table those with the strongest skill sets to help them develop a sophisticated understanding of the literature.

NEW DIRECTIONS FOR HIGHER EDUCATION • DOI: 10.1002/he

Second, in making a decision to act upon results, the expense of implementing change is one important consideration. For example, changes to teaching strategies or assignment to learning communities may yield positive student outcomes, cost little or nothing, and therefore garner wide support. In contrast, before deciding to initiate a brand new academic advising structure complete with building renovations and extensive hiring, administrators must have compelling evidence that outcomes of the project will justify the investment of human and financial resources. Administrators can help build that confidence by understanding the design and rigor of the studies providing supporting evidence, again relying on those with the strongest expertise to build that understanding.

Implications for Administrative Practice

Administrators face many vexing problems without simple or obvious solutions such as student retention declines, low faculty morale, a hostile campus climate, or a weak leadership pipeline. We offer several recommendations to aid administrators in using scholarship to improve professional practice.

Clearly Identify and Define the Problem.   Some problems are readily identifiable such as a decline in applications or student retention. The cause of those problems and solutions for them are complex but the problems can be easy to spot by those tracking data. Other complex problems may hover under the surface, unnoticed or unattended to by many until they boil over into the spotlight. For example, student concerns over the campus racial climate may go unaddressed for a long time before a critical incident or organized protest lights the momentum for change, sometimes resulting in considerable unrest and the ouster of top officials. Campus leaders must expect administrators throughout the organizational hierarchy to identify and report problems and reward them for doing so. Once a problem is identified, a diverse group of campus stakeholders must work together to define it.

Gather Good Data.   In building an understanding of campus problems and contributors to them—part of the first step of the Action Inquiry Model (St. John et al., 2006)—administrators must identify and agree upon specific data sources and data collection procedures and justify those decisions. For example, a decision to consider only first-time, full-time, fall-semester admits in retention models will exclude critical data and obscure the true retention picture. Although it may be more challenging to develop a different student tracking system, doing so will provide a more accurate assessment of retention. Similarly, plenty of evidence supports the role of student involvement and engagement in cocurricular activities in student success but without reliable methods of tracking student participation, administrators and scholars cannot assess its effects. Other ill-structured problems such as campus climate or faculty morale are difficult to assess and those with particular scholarly expertise on those topics must be included in doing so.

Use Theory and Scholarship to Guide Solutions.   Administrators can seek guidance from scholarly literature to solve problems. We have shared models for doing so in this chapter. Using scholarship can help inform administrators by deepening their understanding of complex problems. It can provide new evidence-based strategies for tackling issues. Administrators can use the literature to build a compelling argument and persuade stakeholders on a course of action.

Listen to Skeptics and Critics.   It can be tempting for administrators to surround themselves by like-minded people, but doing so can short-circuit successful implementation of initiatives. Efforts to address one problem may lead to a new problem without careful planning and buy-in. For instance, many on a campus may agree that the funding model for graduate students is unsustainable but disagree in how to best to change it. By gathering a group of bright and committed leaders from various disciplinary backgrounds—including those on the front lines of graduate recruitment and admission—to work together to implement the Action Inquiry Model and devise a funding scheme, the campus is more likely to foster buy-in, maintain and grow enrollment targets, and protect program quality.

Bensimon (2007) posed important questions that reinforce the need to have a wide range of voices at the table as important decisions are made, in this case pertaining to student success:

> When practitioners have been socialized to view student success from the perspective of the dominant paradigm, what do they notice? What might they fail to notice? What do they expect to see and what happens when their expectations are not met? Might the know-how derived from the dominant paradigm be inimical to the needs of minority students? Might it lead to misconceptions? (p. 451)

The failure to include skeptics and critics can contribute to failed strategies and harm to community members.

Learn From Others.   On any given day, administrators can read about serious problems facing postsecondary institutions. Many are typical such as admissions yield rates or student readiness for college. Others may be common but difficult for some to spot, such as issues arising from difficult campus climates or cultures. The report commissioned by Texas A&M University in the wake of the 1999 bonfire collapse that killed 12 and injured 27 offers powerful lessons to campus leaders. In addition to the analysis of the structural failures that led to the collapse, the commission concluded that "a cultural bias impeding risk identification, and the lack of a proactive risk management approach" (Special Commission, 2000, p. 4) contributed to the tragedy. A large body of scholarship exists to aid administrators in understanding campus culture and risk management. It should not take a tragedy or massive protest to invest in developing complex understanding of institutional culture and its influence on the campus community. News reports and in-depth stories from publications such as the *Chronicle of Higher Education* and *Inside Higher Education* ought to prompt administrations to question the relevance of those situations to their own campus and consider opportunities for improvement, identification of risks, and effective response to problems.

Prioritize Professional Development. With so many pressing issues to manage, it can be difficult to prioritize professional development. Theory provides a common language to foster understanding, offers new ways to solve problems, and draws on others' professional wisdom. However, administrators' academic and professional backgrounds vary, so many will need assistance in gaining exposure to and understanding of relevant theories. Utilizing campus experts, bringing scholars and practitioners to campus to teach others, and sending staff to professional meetings are three professional development strategies. Additionally, a common scholarly reading for campus leaders, faculty, and staff will foster discussion and draw upon different academic and professional backgrounds to help solve problems.

Contribute to Scholarship. Finally, administrators should be encouraged to contribute to the literature and supported in doing so. In her discussion of selecting theoretically derived models, Hirschy (2015) urged professionals to consider models embedded in theory and research and then to evaluate results and share information on the effectiveness of their application. With feedback from practitioners, scholars can improve the creation, evaluation, and revision of theories and models.

By presenting on and publishing their findings, administrators can contribute to the iterative cycle of theory development and grow the body of knowledge. They become part of a feedback loop that is essential to improving both scholarship and practice. "Only by applying the formalized scholarly techniques to a local context and by sharing these results broadly can we normalize reflexive practice" (Reason & Kimball, 2012, p. 372).

Conclusion

In this chapter, we reviewed models for apply scholarship to practice and shared recommendations for selecting theoretically derived models. These models and recommendations provide guidance to administrators who seek to be informed by scholarship as they address very complex problems. We also urge those administrators to contribute to the body of knowledge, assisting both scholars and practitioners and muddying the distinction between the two groups.

References

Astin, A. W. (1984). Student involvement: A developmental theory for higher education. *Journal of College Student Personnel, 25*, 297–308.

Bean, J. P., & Metzner, B. S. (1985). A conceptual model of nontraditional undergraduate student attrition. *Review of Educational Research, 55*, 485–540.

Bensimon, E. M. (2007). The underestimated significance of practitioner knowledge in the scholarship on student success. *The Review of Higher Education, 30*, 441–469.

Blimling, G. S. (2011). How are dichotomies such as scholar/practitioner and theory/practice helpful and harmful to the profession? Developing professional judgment. In P. M. Magolda, & M. B. Baxter Magolda (Eds.), *Contested issues in student affairs: Diverse perspectives and respectful dialogue* (pp. 42–53). Sterling, VA: Stylus.

Braxton, J. M. (2014, March). The possibilities of a scholarship of practice. Paper presented at the annual convention of the American College Personnel Association, Indianapolis, IN.

Comeaux, E., & Harrison, K. C. (2011). A conceptual model of academic success for student–athletes. *Educational Researcher, 40*, 235–245.

Hirschy, A. S. (2015). Models of student persistence and retention. In D. Hossler & B. Bontrager (Eds.), *The handbook of strategic enrollment management* (pp. 268–280). San Francisco, CA: Jossey-Bass.

Jones, S. R., Torres, V., & Arminio, J. (2014). *Negotiating the complexities of qualitative research in higher education: Fundamental elements and issues* (2nd ed.). New York, NY: Routledge.

Mayhew, M. J., Rockenbach, A. N., Bowman, N. A., Seifert, T. A., & Wolniak, G. C., with Pascarella, E. T., & Terenzini, P. T. (2016). *How college affects students (Vol. 3): 21st century evidence that higher education works.* San Francisco, CA: Jossey-Bass.

Merton, R. K. (1968). *Social theory and social structure.* New York, NY: The Free Press.

Parker, C. A. (1977). On modeling reality. *Journal of College Student Personnel, 18*, 419–425.

Patton, L. D., Renn, K. A., Guido, F. M., & Quaye, S. J. (2016). *Student development in college: Theory, research, and practice.* San Francisco, CA: Jossey-Bass.

Reason, R. D., & Kimball, E. W. (2012). A new theory-to-practice model for student affairs: Integrating scholarship, context, and reflection. *Journal of Student Affairs Research and Practice, 49*, 359–376.

Reason, R. D., & Kimball, E. W. (2013, March). From theory to practice (and back again). Paper presented at the meeting of ACPA–College Student Educators International, Las Vegas, NV.

Rodgers, R. F., & Widick, C. (1980). Theory to practice: Uniting concepts, logic, and creativity. In F. B. Newton & K. L. Ender (Eds.), *Student development practices: Strategies for making a difference* (pp. 3–25). Springfield, IL: Thomas.

Special Commission on the 1999 Texas A&M Bonfire. (2000, May 2). Final report. Retrieved from http://www.tamu.edu/bonfire-commission/reports/Final.pdf

Stage, F. K. (1994). Fine tuning the instrument: Using process models for work with student development theory. *College Student Affairs Journal, 13*(2), 21–28.

Stage, F. K., & Dannells, M. (2000). *Linking theory to practice: Case studies for working with college students.* Philadelphia, PA: Taylor & Francis.

St. John, E. P., McKinney, J. S., & Tuttle, T. (2006). Using action inquiry to address critical challenges. In E. P. St. John & M. Wilkerson (Eds.), *New Directions for Institutional Research: No. 130. Reframing persistence research to improve academic success* (pp. 63–76). San Francisco, CA: Jossey-Bass.

MAUREEN E. WILSON *is professor and chair of the Department of Higher Education and Student Affairs at Bowling Green State University. She is a senior scholar with ACPA: College Student Educators International.*

AMY S. HIRSCHY *is assistant professor in the College of Education and Human Development at the University of Louisville. She was an academic fellow for the Institute for Higher Education Policy.*

NEW DIRECTIONS FOR HIGHER EDUCATION • DOI: 10.1002/he

4

The chapter considers student engagement to discuss the use of assessment evidence to advance evidence-based practice and to illustrate a scholarship of practice.

The Use of Student Engagement Findings as a Case of Evidence-Based Practice

Jillian Kinzie

In the past two decades, concerns about educational quality coupled with a general skepticism about the value of undergraduate education have intensified, while demands for colleges and universities to demonstrate educational effectiveness and assess outcomes have increased (Burke, 2005; Kuh et al., 2015). At the same time, assessment activities focused on the systematic collection, review, and use of information about educational programs to improve teaching and learning have gained ground in institutional practice (Banta & Palomba, 2015; Kuh et al., 2015). The pressures associated with greater accountability and increased assessment present significant challenges to colleges and universities, demanding measures of educational effectiveness and concerted action using proven methods to improve.

One approach to address current pressures in higher education is for colleges and universities to explicitly apply what research shows matters to student learning and success and, in particular, to use evidence from institutional assessment to guide improvements in undergraduate education. This strategy requires (a) routine application of practical findings from research, (b) attention to institutional evidence about educational effectiveness, and (c) a willingness to use evidence to change the conditions for student learning and success. To put it plainly, lessons from the body of research about what matters to student learning and success must be combined with local evidence about educational effectiveness to inform improvement in undergraduate education.

The strategy just outlined echoes a familiar refrain in higher education: to tighten the connection between educational research and practice (Terenzini, 1996). The notion of bringing research and practice closer together simultaneously requires greater research attention to issues confronting practitioners and practitioners' reliance on evidence-based practice to make changes in undergraduate education. This approach is an expression of what Braxton (2005) defined as a *scholarship of practice*, wherein

NEW DIRECTIONS FOR HIGHER EDUCATION, no. 178, Summer 2017 © 2017 Wiley Periodicals, Inc.
Published online in Wiley Online Library (wileyonlinelibrary.com) • DOI: 10.1002/he.20233

scholarship aims to improve administrative practice and administrative work contributes to the scholarly knowledge base. In particular, the scholarship of practice aims to increase the use of findings of empirical research to develop institutional policy and practice. Further emphasizing the value of practitioner knowledge, Dowd and Tong (2007) emphasized an accountability structure that combines evidence-based decision-making and practitioner inquiry.

The concomitant pressures for accountability and improvement and expansion of assessment in higher education provides an occasion to reflect on the growing body of applied, empirical research that guides practice. This chapter focuses on the 17-year-old assessment project known as the National Survey of Student Engagement (NSSE) to explore evidence-based practice. NSSE's grounding in research associated with desired outcomes in college, assessment objectives, and widespread use makes it ideal for exploring the use of findings of empirical research to guide practice. This chapter considers NSSE's explicit emphasis on assessment to inform practice and guide institutional improvement to discuss the scholarship of practice.

Making the Case for Assessment as Scholarship of Practice

Assessment in higher education is a particular expression of the scholarship of practice. Bred from a combination of applied research and practical institutional interest in understanding educational processes and outcomes, assessment has been cultivated by growing external pressures to empirically demonstrate educational effectiveness and use evidence to improve. Although assessment is a form of educational inquiry that employs quantitative and qualitative research methods, it is generally considered distinct from educational research. Arguing that research and assessment share common processes, Erwin (1991) distinguished assessment as guiding good practice with implications for a single institution, whereas research guides theory and tests concepts with broad implications for higher education. Upcraft and Schuh (2002) emphasize the difference by specifying that while assessment uses research methods, the methods are undertaken to inform practice with the goal of adjusting practice.

Akin to research, assessment aims to answer questions; however, these questions are of a more practical, local concern, such as "to what extent do our students collaborate with peers in class?" or, "how well do our seniors write and what educational practices contribute to the development of students' writing skills?" Findings from assessment help document what works, shape policies, inform decision-making, and guide improvement efforts. More to the point, the goal of assessment is to create changes that improve educational effectiveness and student success.

One of the early scholars of assessment, Barbara Walvoord (2004) defined assessment as a form of "action research," intended not so much to generate theory but to inform local action, adding that because educational contexts involve too many variables to strive for causal explanation, it is more useful to collect indicators and data that can be used in decision-making. The framework of action research is apt, as it emphasizes the wide variety of investigative, evaluative, and analytical methods that can be used to diagnose educational processes and particularly weaknesses and to help educators develop practical solutions. In addition, similar to the predetermined process, or the "cycle of action" followed in action research, assessment is characterized by an "assessment cycle"—an iterative sequence that involves identifying outcomes, collecting and analyzing data, sharing results, identifying and implementing changes, and assessing the impact of change.

Another similarity between action research and assessment is the emphasis on who is involved. Like action research, which is typically conducted by educators working in the institution being studied—rather than by independent researchers—assessment is usually conducted by and at least with faculty, institutional research professionals, and other educators at the college or university. Even more, action research and assessment findings must come to a credible conclusion about what should be done given the findings, which includes thoughtful application to the local context. The emphasis on practitioner inquiry is a key feature of a scholarship of practice that validates practitioners and their influence on decision-making, policy, and practice.

A final important distinction for assessment is that, although it must be done well, using appropriate methods from research, assessment is not judged by research criteria for rigor. Instead, the test for assessment quality is made at a local level, taking into account methodological considerations, as well as organizational and political realities. Upcraft and Schuh (2002) asserted the criterion of "good enough" as a way to gauge assessment. They caution that the failure to understand the differences between research and assessment can result in a "good-enough assessment study being marginalized, trivialized, or ignored because the reader erroneously applies the perfect study syndrome" (p. 20). Blaich and Wise (2011) emphasize that the pursuit of perfect research can distract from assessment's practical aim, whereas the good-enough criterion can motivate action. They suggest that when faced with an assessment study, educators should ask: "Do we have good-enough knowledge to try something different that might benefit our students?" (p. 13). Finally, the emphasis on good enough is not meant to demean high quality assessment nor does it excuse poor studies; rather it underscores the distinguishing quality of assessment: results useful for improvement.

NSSE as a Case of Evidence-Based Practice

The term student engagement emerged in the late 1990s as a framework for understanding, diagnosing, and improving undergraduate education.

Student engagement is a family of constructs that measure the time and energy students devote to educationally purposeful activities—activities that matter to learning and student success (Kuh, 2001). The concept of student engagement and NSSE represent attempts to connect academic research and professional practice—to bring time-honored conceptual and empirical work on college student learning and development to bear on practical matters of higher education assessment and improvement.

Since its first national administration in 2000, more than 1,600 bachelor's-granting colleges and universities have used NSSE to assess educational quality through the lens of effective practice. At the time of its development, higher education was consumed with concerns about college cost escalation, regional accreditors were ratcheting up their demands on colleges and universities to embrace assessment for improvement, and higher education leaders were frustrated by metrics in college rankings (McCormick, Kinzie, & Gonyea, 2013). NSSE introduced a simple reframing of the quality question: Ask undergraduates about their educationally purposeful experiences.

NSSE's focus on measuring students' experiences in educationally purposeful activities is to foster consideration of the robust body of research about what matters to student learning and development. More specifically, the survey emphasizes behaviors positively related to desired learning outcomes and, importantly, outcomes that institutions can influence. The presumption is that by providing participating institutions with comprehensive, easy-to-understand reports about the extent to which their students are engaged relative to those at comparison institutions, NSSE promotes action on results.

Using NSSE Results

The primary goal of NSSE is to make research-based evidence of educational effectiveness and student success relevant to administrators and educators who can use results to assess and improve undergraduate education via pragmatic initiatives including accreditation self-studies, benchmarking and strategic planning, faculty development, retention efforts, state system performance reviews, and more. Every year, about 500 colleges and universities receive NSSE data with the expectation that they will share and make meaning of results, identify priorities for action, formulate action plans, implement those plans, and circle back to assess their impact. This goal and the delivery of results is an example of Braxton's (2005) claim that a scholarship of practice must take "forms of knowledge and make them available and accessible to practitioners" (p. 286). By providing practitioners with local data about practices that matter for student learning, they have a solid basis for action.

From the beginning, NSSE has documented what campuses do with their results. NSSE disseminates institutional examples in annual reports and in three volumes of "Lessons from the Field," and it catalogs examples in an online database (see www.nsse.indiana.edu/html/how_institutions_use_NSSE.cfm). These examples clearly demonstrate that evidence can inform practice and, more importantly, capture the growing body of shared wisdom about the use of results. Collectively, the examples offer concrete illustrations of assessment as a form of scholarship of practice, in particular, the qualities of action research, and reflect Dowd and Tong's (2007) emphasis on a scholarship of practice that integrates evidence and practitioner inquiry.

The following sections document two categories of scholarship of practice using NSSE results—the use of results to inform and improve practice and the development of a knowledge base grounded in evidence and practitioner inquiry.

Using Results to Inform and Improve Practice. Student engagement results help colleges and universities hold themselves accountable for a quality undergraduate experience (McCormick, 2009). Even more, by providing participating institutions with actionable information on student behaviors, NSSE results foster improvement in undergraduate education.

Several institutional examples affirm the use of assessment evidence to inform and improve practice. For instance, in its most recent reaccreditation review with the Middle States Commission on Higher Education, Gettysburg College in Pennsylvania was commended by the visiting team for its exemplary practices of effective, systematic use of indirect assessments, including NSSE, and for improving student learning. The team noted the ways that assessment results brought multiple constituencies into discussions, helped establish new goals and benchmarks, demonstrated achievements in the educational program, and helped make the case for additional resource allocation.

Gettysburg's accreditation success was aided by the fact that NSSE results were regularly reviewed by administrators and faculty, including the President's Council, and the Committee on Institutional Effectiveness. The comprehensiveness of sharing NSSE results helped inform strategic planning on student engagement, in particular to demonstrate and heighten student-faculty interaction. NSSE results affirmed Gettysburg strengths and were used to enhance opportunities for faculty-mentored research, for student travel to professional conferences, and for a new colloquium on undergraduate research. The Gettysburg example exemplifies how accountability can be aided when actionable, reliable evidence is actively considered and acted upon by practitioners.

Assessment results like NSSE that are grounded in extant research about practices that matter for student success are disposed to inform action and improvement in undergraduate education. The provision of a simple data point about collaborative learning, which research shows matters for learning, has catalyzed productive discussions about teaching, assignments, and learning assessments, and enhancements to instructional practice.

A straightforward institutional example of using student engagement data to improve instructional practice is exemplified by the University of North Dakota's (UND) consideration of senior student results on the extent to which students experienced cultural diversity. Seniors' scores on the educational gains include "understanding people of other racial and ethnic backgrounds" and some of the interaction with diversity items were lower than UND desired. Results affirmed the university's decision to modify the general education diversity requirements, and NSSE measures serve as an indicator to gauge the influence of the required courses and curricular adaptations. This example demonstrates the use of evidence to inform changes in policy and practice and the important follow-up to determine if changes are making a difference.

Colleges and universities have brought student engagement results to bear on campus concerns and problems, including declining student persistence rates and the quality of writing. Examples of NSSE data use from Nazareth College in New York and Drake University in Iowa illustrate effective use of results to address campus concerns. Building on faculty and staff discussions of NSSE results to create a campus-wide understanding of the undergraduate experience, and in particular concerns about student persistence, institutional researchers at Nazareth analyzed their NSSE data to compare students who stayed versus those who left. Narrowing this examination to students who left with a 3.0 GPA or better revealed that these students scored low on survey items related to effective teaching and, in particular, the organization of instruction. Faculty discussed these findings and are undertaking a range of responses.

Drake University in Iowa disaggregated results by college and school to recognize pockets of exemplary performance and identify areas in need of improvement. Reports highlighted the top five items in which each unit excelled and the five areas in which they were below peer comparison groups. These custom reports encouraged action by focusing on comparative data in two ways—national benchmarking based on major and internal benchmarking with Drake students across colleges. Results prompted the College of Business and Public Administration, for example, to review its curriculum regarding writing skill development and contributed to changes in the core curriculum. The Nazareth and Drake examples demonstrate the important emphasis in the scholarship of practice to base a study in the issues and concerns confronting practitioners and of the value of incorporating practitioner inquiry.

Developing a Knowledge Base About Acting on Results.   The development of a knowledge base grounded in evidence and practitioner inquiry is another characteristic of a scholarship of practice. NSSE's documentation of data use and analysis of generalizable lessons for practice is illustrated in a systematic review of over 140 institutional NSSE use accounts (Kinzie, Cogswell, & Wheatle, 2015). These stories reveal a range of institutional uses, including using data to inform accreditation processes, improve outcomes including retention, graduation and student success, and contextualize faculty development, among others. This strand of NSSE's work offers evidence of the use of empirical research to inform practice and contributes to the knowledge base about how administrators and faculty actually make decisions from evidence and enact a scholarship of practice.

Several findings from the growing knowledge base about how assessment results from NSSE influence practice demonstrate practical lessons. For example, two essential lessons for the effective use of NSSE data to improve include the importance of reporting results in small, digestible bites to targeted audiences, and the value of first reporting what is working well at the institution and then focusing on areas of improvement by connecting results to topics that hold relevance (i.e., first-year retention, program review, and advising). Another lesson highlights the importance of evidence to bring practitioners together to discuss issues confronting the campus and to consider change. NSSE results provide an occasion to bring faculty, staff, and students into a conversation about undergraduate quality and topics of campus concern and to address: "what do we want to do with and about these results?" And even better, "what's next?"

Finally, the examination of accounts about how NSSE data are used suggest that action on evidence is rarely achieved through mandates or simply by participating in a survey and sharing results. Instead, it is through thoughtful planning about with whom to share results, the creation of customized reports, and the intentional use of evidence by committed educators that campus conversations and timely action can happen. The development of a knowledge base of practical examples and lessons about the connection between research, evidence, and practice and how to make change in undergraduate education is an important aspect of the scholarship of practice.

Student Engagement and Practice-Oriented Research

A secondary NSSE objective is to promote empirical research. Scholars affiliated with the project regularly conduct studies using the NSSE dataset, and these findings are featured in journals and in NSSE Annual Results reports 2000–2016 (see www.nsse.indiana.edu/html/annual_results.cfm). In 2015, for example, survey findings indicated that many students are not challenged to do their best work and course challenge bears little relation to admission selectivity, suggesting that faculty need to invest in designing course assignments that prompt students to put forth their best effort and that selectivity does not guarantee challenging academic experiences (National Survey of Student Engagement, 2015). This sort of research using assessment data follows a more traditional form of scholarship and also affirms research on practical educational concerns.

Scholarship conducted by administrators in NSSE-participating colleges and universities, institutional research professionals, and researchers working in national higher education organizations such as the Association for American Colleges and Universities (AAC&U) demonstrates the range of scholars who can contribute to a practice-oriented knowledge base. This section highlights a few examples of practice-oriented scholarship.

Building on Kuh's (2008) findings on the educational significance of high-impact practices (HIPs) for historically underserved students, Finley and McNair (2013) examined equity and the cumulative effects of student participation in HIPs—including service-learning, undergraduate research, internships, and culminating experiences. Analyzing NSSE data from 38 campuses in California, Oregon, and Wisconsin, Finley and McNair advance collective understanding, showing for example, that there is a positive relationship between students' cumulative participation in multiple high-impact practices and engagement in deep learning and perceived educational gains. Importantly, their work is aimed at campus practitioners, combining quantitative and qualitative approaches to provide an inquiry-based methodological model for campus practitioners to support purposeful and intentional study as well as equitable implementation of high-impact practices at institutions.

The identification of predictors for student success among students at a particular institution provides insightful modeling and allows for tailored approaches to improvement. Institutional researchers and administrators at Indiana University Bloomington, for example, conducted a predictive analysis using six years of NSSE data and student academic records to understand how student engagement relates to first-year retention, academic performance, and timely graduation (Fiorini, Liu, Shepard, & Ouimet, 2014). The study identified actionable elements of student engagement, including working hard to meet faculty's expectations, writing medium and long papers, and participating in co-curricular activities, among others, to inform the adjustment of existing programs and the development of new programs to support student success. Results from this institutional study provided useful local understandings regarding what contributes to student success.

In another example of faculty analyzing NSSE data to inform practice, Popkess and McDaniel (2011) explored student engagement among nursing students and in relation to preprofessional groups, education, and other health-majors. Findings that nursing majors were more academically challenged and engaged in rigorous curricula, but that they engaged less in active and collaborative learning than other preprofessional groups suggested the need to work with faculty to increase opportunities for students to contribute to class discussions and work with other students in/out of class.

The opportunity to conduct in-depth studies using NSSE data to explore real campus concerns including student persistence and qualitative differences among student groups, and to use this information to guide practice and policy in colleges and universities, demonstrates the potential for tightening the connection between research and practice.

Final Thoughts on NSSE and the Scholarship of Practice

The concept of student engagement in effective educational practice is a practical representation of the robust body of research about what matters to student learning and success. When campuses ground the design of environments, programs, practices, and policies to promote student engagement, they are effectively using empirical research to guide practice.

The objective of bridging academic research and practice is enhanced and deepened when administrators, faculty, and staff have their own institutional assessment data about the extent to which students are engaged. Equipped with accessible, understandable evidence about student behaviors and institutional conditions, colleges and universities can use their assessment results to develop and refine policy and practice. The increased use of student engagement research to guide practice and greater reliance on institutional assessment evidence about student engagement to inform campus decision-making and planning is an expression of the foundational principles of a scholarship of practice.

Institutions that truly *use* NSSE—as distinguished from merely participating in it—know that the receipt of data files and reports is only the beginning of a process of sharing and making meaning of results, identifying priorities for action, formulating concrete action plans, implementing those plans, and circling back to assess their impact. To enhance undergraduate education for all, it is critical that administrators and faculty dedicate greater attention to using empirical research and assessment results as a foundation for developing institutional policy and data-informed improvement initiatives in colleges and universities. By doing so, administrators and faculty demonstrate their participation in the scholarship of practice.

References

Banta, T. W., & Palomba, C. A. (2015). *Assessment essentials: Planning, implementing, and improving assessment in higher education* (2nd ed.). San Francisco, CA: Jossey-Bass.

Blaich, C., & Wise, K. (2011). *From gathering to using assessment results: Lessons from the Wabash national study*. Occasional Paper #8. Champaign, IL: National Institute for Learning Outcomes Assessment.

Braxton, J. M. (2005). Reflections on a scholarship of practice. *The Review of Higher Education, 28*(2), 285–293.

Burke, J. C. (2005). The many faces of accountability. In J. C. Burke et al. (Eds.), *Achieving accountability in higher education* (pp. 1–24). San Francisco, CA: Jossey-Bass.

Dowd, A. C., & Tong, V. P. (2007). Accountability, assessment, and the scholarship of "best practice." In J. C. Smart (Ed.), *Handbook of higher education* (Vol. 22, pp. 57–119). Dordrecht, The Netherlands: Springer.

Erwin, T. D. (1991).*Assessing student learning and development: A guide to principles, goals, and methods of determining college outcomes*. San Francisco, CA: Jossey-Bass.

Finley, A., & McNair, T. (2013). *Assessing underserved students' engagement in high-impact practices*. Washington, DC: Association of American Colleges and Universities.

Fiorini, S., Liu, T. Shepard, L., & Ouimet, J. (2014). *Using NSSE to understand student success: A multi-year analysis*. Proceedings of the 10th Annual National Symposium on Student Retention, The University of Oklahoma.

Kinzie, J., Cogswell, C.A., & Wheatle, K.I. (2015). Reflections on the state of student engagement data use and strategies for action. *Assessment Update, 27*(2), 1–2; 14–16.

Kuh, G. D. (2001). Assessing what really matters to student learning: Inside the National Survey of Student Engagement. *Change, 33*(3), 10–17.

Kuh, G. D. (2008). *High-impact educational practices: What they are, who has access to them, and why they matter*. Washington, DC: Association of American Colleges and Universities.

Kuh, G. D., Ikenberry, S. O., Jankowski, N., Cain, T. R., Ewell, P. T., Hutchings, P., & Kinzie, J. (2015). *Using evidence of student learning to improve higher education*. San Francisco, CA: Jossey-Bass.

McCormick, A. C. (2009). Toward reflective accountability. In R. M. Gonyea & G. D. Kuh (Eds.), *New directions for institutional research: No. 141. Using NSSE in institutional research* (pp. 97–106). Hoboken, NJ: Wiley.

McCormick, A. C., Kinzie, J., & Gonyea, R. M. (2013). Student engagement: Bridging research and practice to improve the quality of undergraduate education. In M. B. Paulsen (Ed.), *Higher education: Handbook of theory and research* (Vol. 28, pp. 47–92). Dordrecht, The Netherlands: Springer.

National Survey of Student Engagement. (2015). *Engagement insights: Survey findings on the quality of undergraduate education—annual results 2015*. Bloomington: Indiana University Center for Postsecondary Research.

Popkess, A., & McDaniel, A. (2011). Are nursing students engaged in learning? A secondary analysis of data from the national survey of student engagement. *Nursing Education Perspectives, 32*(2), 89–94.

Terenzini, P. T. (1996). Rediscovering roots: Public policy and higher education research. *The Review of Higher Education, 20*(1), 5–13.

Upcraft, L., & Schuh, J. (2002). Assessment vs. research: Why we should care about the difference. *About Campus, 7*(1), 6–20.

Walvoord, B. (2004). *Assessment clear and simple: A practical guide for institutions, departments, and general education*. San Francisco, CA: Jossey-Bass.

JILLIAN KINZIE is associate director at the Indiana University School of Education Center for Postsecondary Research and the NSSE Institute.

5

This chapter will construct a prototype of a scholarship of practice through specific application to general education. The chapter includes specific illustrations and potential challenges for such an endeavor.

Constructing a Prototype: Realizing a Scholarship of Practice in General Education

Cynthia A. Wells

Why a scholarship of practice? Toward what end do we assess the merits of such a concept? John Braxton (2003) recommends a scholarship of practice as a means to enhance the utility of empirical research by developing and refining knowledge that improves institutional policy and practice in higher education. In essence, a scholarship of practice turns the scholarly assets of the academy on the work of the academy itself.

The notion engages the ideas of *Scholarship Reconsidered* (Boyer, 1990) in a manner that sets a vision for scholar-practitioners in higher education. The scholarship of practice applies the "original indicators of excellence for the scholarly profession" to administrative leadership (p. 16). That is, to "think well, continuously learn, reflect upon inquiry, identify connections, build bridges between theory and practice, and communicate one's knowledge effectively" characterizes excellence in higher education administration (p. 16). As such, the scholarship of practice offers a means to institutional effectiveness.

The notion of a scholarship of practice is opportune. Outlining the specific elements of such an endeavor is particularly beneficial as the notion of scholar-practitioner is an outcome commonly espoused in the mission statements of higher education graduate programs (Freeman, Hagedorn, Goodchild, & Wright, 2013). Moreover, institutional effectiveness is the central concern of regional accrediting bodies (Higher Learning Commission, 2015; Middle States Commission on Higher Education, 2006; New England Association of Schools and Colleges, 2015; Southern Association of Colleges and Schools, 2013; Western Association of Schools and Colleges, 2013). Finally, whether colleges and universities are fulfilling their promises

New Directions for Higher Education, no. 178, Summer 2017 © 2017 Wiley Periodicals, Inc.
Published online in Wiley Online Library (wileyonlinelibrary.com) • DOI: 10.1002/he.20234

is a primary concern of the public (Bennett & Wilezol, 2013; Selingo, 2013). As with all new notions, it is crucial to build a compelling narrative advocating such a vision, clarifying parameters, clearly articulating the connection of a scholarship of practice to previous conceptions, and providing evidence for the benefit of its adoption. Building a compelling argument for a scholarship of practice depends, at least in part, on demonstrating its utility in specific contexts.

This chapter will argue that general education exemplifies a higher education context in which a scholarship of practice is both necessary and generative. After querying "why" general education is a valuable context for a scholarship of practice, this chapter turns to how such a scholarship ideal honors Boyer's (1990) original intentions for reconsidering scholarship. How a scholarship of practice might be realized in general education, including specific illustrations and potential challenges facing such an endeavor, will then be considered. On the whole, this chapter will construct a prototype of a scholarship of practice through specific application to general education.

Why General Education Is a Valuable Context for a Scholarship of Practice

A scholarship of practice is particularly relevant in contexts in which higher education leaders are conducting work in uncharted waters. The vast majority of college and university leaders have not been trained specifically for their administrative work (Braxton, 2003); general education oversight is no exception. General education administrators are typically experts in a particular academic discipline, and must learn how to oversee a shared interdisciplinary and/or cross-disciplinary curriculum through on-the-job experience. This requires both considering existing literature and sometimes pursuing one's own inquiry in order to comprehend theoretical frameworks and refine general education programs. The work of general education curricula, from foundational premises to course design to program assessment, is intellectual work, requiring the same kinds of focus and concentration that faculty apply in other realms (Hanstedt, 2012). Seeing the ideals of general education within a framework of a scholarship of practice helps higher education leaders realize the rigor and benefit of this proposition.

General education also aligns with the framework for a scholarship of practice by illustrating how the development of a generative knowledge base guides educational practice and shapes institutional policy. General education design and implementation benefits from knowledge regarding its theoretical foundations, socio-historical context, and avenues to institutional change. As one example, Zayed's (2012) examination of general education reforms in the mid-20th century at Michigan State University identified a wide variety of factors in both institutional and national contexts that influenced the content and process of curricular change. Higher education

NEW DIRECTIONS FOR HIGHER EDUCATION • DOI: 10.1002/he

leaders benefit from incisive analysis into which models of general education work in specific institutional contexts.

Furthermore, administrative practice related to general education benefits from understanding student and faculty perceptions and experiences with general education in order to facilitate deeper engagement and advance learning outcomes. For example, Hall, Culver, and Burge (2012) sought to better comprehend student perceptions of both the level of importance placed upon, as well as satisfaction with, general education. Moreover, these scholars investigated connections between student perceptions of general education learning outcomes and faculty teaching practices. The contributions to the knowledge base impact not only students and faculty at a given college or university but also help a wide audience of higher education scholar-practitioners when extended more broadly to scholarly literature.

Moreover, the administrative work of general education needs a framework for excellence, which is offered by a scholarship of practice. Building on Boyer's (1990) expansive but largely conceptual vision of scholarship, Glassick, Huber, and Maeroff (1997) clarified these six standards for excellence: clarity of aims, adequate preparation, methods that match queries, results that reflect analytical rigor, effective communication and description of results, as well as reflective critique of the work. Hutchings' and Shulman's (1999) framework for determining what rises to the level of scholarship is equally beneficial. They argue that to be considered scholarship, the work must meet three criteria: It must be made public, be available for peer review and critique according to accepted standards, and be able to be replicated and built on by other scholars. These standards suitably determine excellence in scholarly activities that improve policy and practice in general education.

Applying these criteria for excellence to general education illustrates the value of a scholarship of practice in this realm of higher education administration. A scholarship base in general education that effectively guides practice requires conceptual clarity and interpretive acuity. There are a wide variety of implicit ideals for general education evident in our society and institutions (Wells, 2016b). These ideals must be analyzed and clarified if we are to comprehend and examine them accurately. A scholarship of practice for general education requires adequate preparation in that administrators must have a comprehensive grasp of the literature, including empirical examinations of general education, national conversations on the perceived importance (or lack thereof) of general education, as well as specific institutional history. General education is incredibly complex; its outcomes include skills and content knowledge as well as qualities and values, and advancing scholarly understanding requires analytical rigor and precision as well as methods that match specific queries. For the results of research on general education to be useful in improving programs and practices both within and across institutional contexts, effective communication of results is paramount. Finally, the scholarship of practice for general education requires reflective critique in order to improve administrative practice within and beyond specific curricular contexts (Palomba, 2002). These ideals for excellence must be employed if we are to navigate our way to improving policy and practice.

Finally, general education fits the framework for a scholarship of practice in that it exemplifies how a knowledge base depends on a scholarly division of labor (Braxton, 2003). In the particular context of general education, questions can be addressed by a variety of groups, including higher education faculty, general education administrators, and institutional researchers. Leaders serving in statewide coordinating boards synthesize data and develop statewide policy related to general education in cross-institutional contexts (Pennsylvania State System of Higher Education, 2014; Texas Higher Education Coordinating Board, 2015). Scholars serving in national higher education organizations such as the Association of American Colleges and Universities contribute to a practice-oriented knowledge base regarding content, methods, models, and pathways to general education (Ferren & Kinch, 2003; Hanstedt, 2016; Humphreys, 2016; Leskes & Wright, 2005). General education not only benefits from, but, indeed, requires, a scholarly division of labor.

Clearly, general education fits the framework espoused for a scholarship of practice. In addition to meeting Braxton's (2003) criteria, a scholarship of practice in general education honors Boyer's (1990) initial intensions for proposing a more expansive view of scholarship.

How Scholarship of Practice in General Education Honors the Intentions of an Expanded Scholarly Vision

Some of the central concerns that drove arguments in *Scholarship Reconsidered* (Boyer, 1990) are germane to general education today. Priorities in American higher education were "significantly realigned" in the mid 20th century as the focus shifted "from the student to the professoriate, from general to specialized education, and from loyalty to the campus to loyalty to the profession" (p. 13). In that era, general education models that are based on providing students various slices of disciplinary pie came to prominence (Harvard University, 1945). General education models across institutional types moved from predominantly shared content models to distribution models to accommodate the desires of faculty who valued specialization. Distribution models allowed faculty to teach within their discipline and to have their introductory courses "count" as general education. The problem was not faculty specialization per se but, rather, that this specialization emphasis was overwhelming all institutions. The distribution model took precedence even when institutional mission might have dictated a focus on general education as a shared, interdisciplinary model.

In making the case for this new vision of scholarship, Boyer (1990) raised three fundamental queries that are fully applicable to general education. The first question was, "Can we have a higher education system in this country that includes multiple models of success" (Boyer, 1990, p. 2). Boyer's concern was that "the research mission, which was appropriate for *some* institutions, created a shadow over the entire learning enterprise" (p. 12). In asking whether U.S. higher education had the capacity for multiple models of success, Boyer was advocating for indicators of institutional excellence that extend beyond traditional research. Boyer's (1990) underlying concern was that campus priorities had become "more imitative than distinctive" (p. 2). General education is too often imitative, adopting models from other institutions without regard for the borrowing institution's distinct purposes and how a general education design advances those context-specific aims. This is not to say that adopting effective educational practices from other institutions is inherently ill-thought-out; rather, it is to say that adopting any educational practice without the careful, thoughtful effort to do so coherently and in light of institutional distinctiveness is misguided.

The second question, "Can the work of our colleges and universities become more "intellectually coherent?" is equally vital to general education (Boyer, 1990). The concern about whether colleges and universities are educationally coherent is as valid today as it was a quarter century ago. A longitudinal analysis of general education indicates that coherence remains elusive (Boning, 2007). Nonetheless, general education is regularly touted as a means to coherence in today's academy (Wells, 2016b). The connection between general education and the intellectual coherence of the academy is a crucial, ongoing concern.

The third question about whether America's colleges can be of "greater service to the nation and the world" is also essential to general education (Boyer, 1990, p. 2). General education is often a space in which learning outcomes related to service and social responsibility are advanced, and general education requirements enable students to wrestle with societal challenges (Allen, 2006). Moreover, general education programs include specific requirements and pedagogies, such as service learning, that are implemented in order to advance students' capacities for serving the common good.

In addition to suiting the concerns that animated early work in expanding spheres of scholarship, effective general education also reflects the interconnectedness of the scholarly functions in ways that signal the value of a scholarship of practice. The scholarship of discovery, integration, application, and teaching were conceptualized as "four separate, yet overlapping, functions" rather than divergent spheres (Boyer, 1990, p. 16). They were conceived holistically as elements that overlap and interact, not as discrete elements, and are better viewed as an operating system than as a list of disconnected options (Boshier, 2009). Unfortunately, these domains have too often been separated (Boshier, 2009; Wells, 2016a). As such, to create a prototype of a scholarship of practice for general education, it is important that we examine the domains of scholarship individually but also that we reexamine their interconnectedness.

A Scholarship of Practice for General Education

What would it look like to use theoretically grounded scholarship to develop institutional policy and practice as it relates to general education? This section addresses this query by briefly summarizing the four types of scholarship, providing examples and illustrations of their adoption in various general education contexts, and then reflects on their interconnectedness when used to support a knowledge base for effective general education practice and policy.

Scholarship of Discovery

The scholarship of discovery is associated with empirical research, that is a "systematic process of collecting, analyzing and interpreting information (data) in order to increase our understanding of a phenomenon" (Leedy & Ormrod, 2010, p. 2). By its very nature, discovery is focused, contributing to our body of knowledge through a detailed understanding of one isolated aspect of reality.

The scholarship of discovery, in many ways, animates academic life. It contributes not only to the advancement of knowledge but also to the intellectual climate of a college or university (Boyer, 1990). The intellectual excitement fueled by the quest to expand our knowledge base invigorates both faculty and higher learning institutions.

The scholarship of discovery fully pertains to general education and thus supports a scholarship of practice. Genuine discovery in the general education context is absolutely crucial. As one illustration, Mahoney and Schamber (2011) investigated how students' emerging knowledge regarding the value of liberal education impacted their sense of self. The research question alone is germane to general education in that it considers both an ideal associated with general education (i.e., liberal education) but also examines specific learning outcomes related to general education (i.e., views of the self). The scholarly context further extends the application to general education in that these researchers examined these questions within the context of a learning community that linked a first-year interdisciplinary seminar with a course in public speaking; both courses fulfilled requirements in the institution's general education curriculum.

Researchers analyzed student speeches on the value of liberal education, an assignment that required students to read and discuss texts on both epistemology and liberal education. The researchers found that students advanced in their capacity to develop and own their points of view as well as to ask good questions. Furthermore, the researchers noted that students gained "deep understanding of the potential of a liberal education" as it related not only to advancing their career but also to advancing transformative personal change and helping them derive "meaning from their lives" (Mahoney & Schamber, 2011, p. 242). This new knowledge provides insight into general education-related student learning outcomes including conceptions of liberal education and views of the self. It also contributes to our knowledge base about what educational practices and pedagogies advance student learning in a general education context.

Scholarship of Integration. The scholarship of integration builds on the scholarship of discovery by extending the meaning and comprehension of original research (Glassick, 2000). The scholarship of integration entails discerning patterns and shedding new insight on research findings (Boyer, 1990; Braxton, 2003). The scholarship of integration involves making interdisciplinary connections, placing the specialties in larger context, and illuminating data in revealing ways. The scholarship of integration often demands interdisciplinary collaboration and requires that the critical analysis of knowledge be followed by creative synthesis in such a way that what is known speaks to specific issues. Moreover, a scholarship of integration shifts our primary focus from a specialist to a nonspecialist audience (Boyer, 1990).

The scholarship of integration is an especially relevant domain of scholarship for general education. General education takes existing knowledge and shares it with a nonspecialist audience in a manner that helps put knowledge in context. General education administration also depends on a scholarship of integration for pulling together seemingly disparate knowledge and methodologies into a coherent educational program. Educating nonspecialists is at the heart of general education.

As one instance, integrating knowledge from the existing research literature with reflection on practice enabled a team of scholars to discern critical themes regarding what constitutes effective leadership in the context of general education renewal (Gano-Phillips et al., 2011). The team examined general education renewal processes in three distinct institutional contexts that used three different reform methods; the subsequent insights were considered in connection with the broader literature regarding effective general education reform. Three underlying themes were identified as critical to leadership in general education reform: collaboration in leadership, developing trust among constituents, and adopting a posture of institutional stewardship. The painstaking work of examining three different methods for enacting change in multiple contexts in light of the larger literature provided crucial new insights into good practice for leadership in general education reform.

The benefits of a scholarship of integration in a context of administrative practice are also evident in this illustration. Gaff (2007) notes that the work that faculty conduct in leading educational innovation lacks "academic currency" (p. 12); a scholarship of practice that embodies the ideals of a scholarship of integration illustrates the conceptualization and theory-building that goes into institutional reform. Moreover, general education reform is notoriously challenging (Gaston & Gaff, 2009). A scholarship of practice signifies the meticulous effort of data gathering, analysis, reflection, synthesis, and dissemination that undergirds effective general education reform.

Scholarship of Engagement.   The scholarship of engagement, which evolved from the original notion of a scholarship of application, entails applying knowledge in order to address societal concerns. The scholarship of engagement draws on disciplinary expertise, connects with audiences external to the campus, and bridges academic work with community needs (Checkoway, 2002). Reciprocal relationships between the academy and community undergird the scholarship of engagement (Ward, 2003); the scholarship of engagement serves the community and also advances academic work.

General education is ripe with opportunities to improve policy and practice through a scholarship of engagement. General education requires applying knowledge to social issues of consequence and teaching in ways that help students engage in their world. In fact, the question of what society needs from an educated person has long been at the heart of general education (Cohen & Kiskar, 2010; Harvard University, 1945).

As an exemplar, Schamber and Mahoney (2008) sought to understand the civic learning outcomes associated with a short-term community engagement experience in the context of a first-year course embedded in an interdisciplinary general education curriculum. A hybrid design that included both quantitative and qualitative dimensions enabled the researchers to advance knowledge in two ways. The quantitative aspect of the study demonstrated student gains in political awareness and social justice attitudes. The qualitative aspect of the study provided insight into students' capacity for civic engagement. Position papers were critically and collaboratively analyzed, revealing that students' increased "empathetic awareness of acute needs of critical populations" and gained "insight into injustices involving sociological disparities" (Shamber & Mahoney, 2008, p. 93). Intellectual insight was brought to bear on actual student learning.

This work embodies the scholarship of engagement by bridging academic needs with community needs. This research illuminates how institutional practice advances what Saltmarsh (2005) identified as the primary aim for first-year students in a general education context as it relates to civic learning; specifically, students' capacity for civic engagement including associated knowledge, skills, and values associated with that learning is a developmentally and educationally appropriate learning outcome in this context. Researchers' critical reflection as well as dissemination of their findings filled a gap in our knowledge base on civic education in a general education curricular context.

Scholarship of Teaching and Learning.   Finally, the scholarship of teaching and learning (Boshier, 2009), building on Boyer's (1990) original framing as the scholarship of teaching, views classrooms and other learning spaces as sites for inquiry and knowledge-building (Bishop-Clark & Dietz-Uhler, 2012). Faculty closely and critically examine student learning in order to improve their courses and programs and also disseminate these insights so that colleagues can evaluate and build on new knowledge (Hutchings, Huber, & Ciccone, 2011). Braxton, Luckey, and Helland (2002) delineate the scholarship of teaching and learning as the development and improvement of pedagogical practice. As such, the scholarship of teaching and learning connects pedagogical conversations in and across institutions and disciplinary fields in order to improve teaching practices in higher education.

The scholarship of teaching and learning is crucial to general education. Teaching disciplinary content such as sociology, psychology, or history to a nonspecialist audience requires distinct teaching models and methods (Handstedt, 2012). Similarly, teaching in an interdisciplinary context requires suitable pedagogies and practices. To be effective in advancing intended general education learning outcomes, such courses need to be designed and delivered differently than if the course were targeted to specialists in a discipline. The scholarship of teaching and learning contributes to general education practice and policy by exploring what models and pedagogies advance general education learning outcomes.

As an illustration, Olsen, Bekken, McConnell, and Walter (2011) conducted a comprehensive examination of an experimental general education curriculum in the context of a large, public, research university. The two-year, thematic general education curriculum incorporated assumptions associated with a constructivist paradigm of learning into the course content, pedagogy, and curricular structure. The researchers found that this teaching practice enhanced student investment in class dialogue and made a positive impact on students' ability to raise insightful questions and make meaningful connections. Furthermore, their study found that faculty posture shifted from a teaching-centered to a learner-centered paradigm. This study illustrates how the scholarship of teaching and learning is critical to better understanding how curricular design and implementation is more effective when based on a knowledge base that addresses how students learn in general education contexts.

Although it is clear that general education offers an administrative context that illustrates the benefits of a scholarship of practice, it is equally critical to be mindful of the interconnections across the four spheres of scholarship and how these interconnections are manifest in a scholarship of practice for general education. The knowledge base associated with the scholarship of teaching and learning, for example, is the product of discovery, integration, and engagement combining as "active ingredients of a dynamic and iterative teaching process" (Boshier 2009, p. 5). Dynamic teaching is context laden; good teaching in upper level disciplinary courses requires different knowledge and delivery skills than interdisciplinary or introductory-level disciplinary courses that fulfill general education requirements. The scholarship of integration bridges various aspects of discovery in order to synthesize what is known, not only to gain new insights but also to communicate with different audiences. And finally, discovery, integration, and teaching merge to build a scholarship of engagement in which students learn to apply knowledge to real-world problems. The interconnections across the four scholarship domains are crucial to a scholarship of practice that endeavors to improve general education.

Conclusion

By their very definition, prototypes represent some compromise from the realized production design. Proposing general education as a prototype presupposes the need for further refinement and retooling for a scholarship of practice. The ultimate design will fulfill the primary goals of a scholarship of practice, which are the improvement of administrative practice in higher education and the development of a knowledge base worthy of rigorous administrative work.

In laying out a prototype, it is important to be mindful of the challenges associated with general education as an opportunity for the scholarship of practice. In addition to positive parallels between a scholarship of practice and general education, there are shared limitations of general education and the typology. It has been widely bemoaned that "scholarship reconsidered" lacked definitional clarity (Boshier, 2009; Glassick, 2000; Hutchings & Shulman, 1999; Wells, 2016a) even as it offered a rich vocabulary and valuable conceptual anchor (Glassick, 2000; Wells, 2016a). Unfortunately, general education also suffers from longstanding conceptual confusion (Wells, 2016b). Moreover, a wide variety of scholarly products are devoted to general education; the illustrations used in this chapter alone span from scholarly articles to empirical research, reflective essays to position-taking rhetorical discourse. It is critical to be attentive to precise meaning and to influences of form in moving from prototype to implemented model.

At its core, a scholarship of practice revolves around the idea of theoretically grounded research findings being used to develop institutional policy and practice (Braxton, 2003). By adopting the scholarship of practice to general education, we can creatively identify the meaning and purpose of a scholarship of practice even as we improve the work of general education itself.

References

Allen, M. J. (2006). *Assessing general education programs*. San Francisco, CA: Jossey-Bass.
Bennett, W., & Wilezol, D. (2013). *Is college worth it: A former United States secretary of education and a liberal arts graduate expose the broken promise of higher education*. Nashville, TN: Thomas Nelson.

Bishop-Clark, C., & Dietz-Uhler, B. (2012). *Engaging in the scholarship of teaching and learning: A guide to the process, and how to develop a project from start to finish.* Sterling, VA: Stylus Press.

Boning, K. (2007). Coherence in general education: A historical look. *Journal of General Education, 56*(1), 1–16.

Boshier, R. (2009). Why is the scholarship of teaching and learning such a hard sell? *Higher Education Research & Development, 28*(1), 1–15.

Boyer, E. L. (1990). *Scholarship reconsidered: Priorities of the professoriate.* Princeton, NJ: Carnegie Foundation for the Advancement of Teaching.

Braxton, J. (2003). *Reflections on a scholarship of practice.* Presidential address delivered at the Association of the Study of Higher Education conference, Portland, OR.

Braxton, J., Luckey, W., & Helland, P. (2002). Institutionalizing a broader view of scholarship through Boyer's four domains. *ASHE-ERIC Higher Education Report, 29*(2). San Francisco, CA: Jossey-Bass.

Checkoway, B. (2002). *Creating the engaged campus.* Presentation at the annual meeting of the American Association for Higher Education, Faculty Roles and Rewards Conference, Phoenix, AZ.

Cohen, A., & Kiskar, C. (2010). *The shaping of American higher education: Emergence and growth of the contemporary system* (2nd ed.). San Francisco, CA: Jossey-Bass.

Ferren, A., & Kinch, A. (2003). The dollars and sense behind general education reform. *Peer Review, 5*(4), 8–11.

Freeman, S. Jr., Hagedorn, L. S., Goodchild, L., & Wright, D. (2013). *Advancing higher education as a field of study: In quest of doctoral degree guidelines—Commemorating 120 years of excellence.* Sterling, VA: Stylus.

Gaff, J. (2007). What if the faculty really do assume responsibility for the educational program? *Liberal Education, 93*(4), 6–13.

Gano-Phillips, S., Barnett, R. W., Kelsh, A., Hawthorne, J., Mitchell, N. D., & Jonson, J. (2011). Rethinking the role of leadership in general education. *Journal of General Education, 60*(2), 65–83.

Gaston, P. L., & Gaff, J. (2009). *Revising general education—and avoiding the potholes.* Washington DC: American Association of Colleges and Universities.

Glassick, C. G. (2000). Boyer's expanded definitions of scholarship, the standards for assessing scholarship, and the elusiveness of the scholarship of teaching. *Academic Medicine, 75,* 877–880.

Glassick, C. E., Huber, M. Y., & Maeroff, G. I. (1997). *Scholarship assessed: Evaluation of the professoriate.* An Ernest L. Boyer Project of The Carnegie Foundation for the Advancement of Teaching. San Francisco, CA: Jossey-Bass.

Hall, M. R., Culver, S. M., & Burge, P. L. (2012). Faculty teaching practices as predictors of student satisfaction with a general education curriculum. *Journal of General Education, 61*(4), 352–368.

Hanstedt, P. (2012). *General education essentials: A guide for college faculty.* San Francisco, CA: Jossey-Bass.

Hanstedt, P. (2016). Reconsidering our definition of the "whole student": An argument for an authority-based approach to university education. *Liberal Education, 102*(3), 58–63.

Harvard University, Committee on the Objectives of a General Education in a Free Society. (1945). *General education in a free society: Report of the Harvard committee.* Cambridge, MA: Harvard University Press.

Higher Learning Commission. (2015). *Criteria and core components.* Retrieved from https://www.hlcommission.org/Criteria-Eligibility-and-Candidacy/criteria-and-core-components.html

Humphreys, D. (2016). Progress and prospects for the reform of undergraduate education: Results from the latest survey of AACU members. *Liberal Education, 102*(3), 28–35.

Hutchings, P., Huber, M., & Ciccone, A. (2011). *The scholarship of teaching and learning reconsidered: Institutional integration and impact.* San Francisco, CA: Jossey-Bass.

Hutchings, P., & Shulman, L. S. (1999). The scholarship of teaching: New elaborations, new developments. *Change 31*(5), 10–15.

Leedy, P. D., & Ormrod, J. E. (2010). *Practical research: Planning and design* (9th ed.). Boston, MA: Pearson Education.

Leskes, A., & Wright, B. D. (2005). *The art and science of assessment general education outcomes: A practical guide.* Washington DC: Association of American Colleges and Universities.

Mahoney, S., & Schamber, J. (2011). Integrative and deep learning through a learning community: A process view of self. *Journal of General Education, 60*(4), 234–247.

Middle States Commission on Higher Education. (2006). *Characteristics of excellence in higher education: Requirements of affiliation and standards for accreditation.* Retrieved from http://www.msche.org/publications/CHX-2011-WEB.pdf

New England Association of Schools and Colleges. (2015). *Standards for accreditation.* Retrieved from https://cihe.neasc.org/standards-policies/standards-accreditation

Olsen, D., Bekken, B. M., McConnell, K. D., & Walter, C. T. (2011). Teaching for change: Learning partnerships and epistemological growth. *Journal of General Education, 60*(3), 139–171.

Palomba, C. A. (2002). Scholarly assessment of student learning in the major and general education. In T. W. Banta (Ed.), *Building a scholarship of assessment* (pp. 201–222). San Francisco, CA: Jossey-Bass.

Pennsylvania State System of Higher Education. (2014). *Strategic plan 2020: Rising to the challenge.* Retrieved from http://www.passhe.edu/inside/bog/Documents/Strategic%20Plan%202020%20Rising%20to%20the%20Challenge_6-16.pdf

Saltmarsh, J. (2005). The civic promise of service learning. *Liberal Education, 91*(2), 50–55.

Schamber, J. F., & Mahoney, S. L. (2008). The development of political awareness and social justice citizenship through community-based learning in a first-year general education seminar. *The Journal of General Education, 57*(2), 75–99.

Selingo, J. (2013). *College (un)bound: The future of higher education and what it means for students.* Boston, MA: New Harvest.

Southern Association of Colleges and Schools. (2013). *The principles of accreditation: Foundations for quality enhancement.* Retrieved from http://www.sacscoc.org/pdf/2012PrinciplesOfAcreditation.pdf

Texas Higher Education Coordinating Board. (2015). *60X30TX, Texas higher education strategic plan.* Retrieved from http://www.thecb.state.tx.us/reports/PDF/6862.PDF?CFID=42058138&CFTOKEN=69598054

Ward, K. (2003). *Faculty service roles and the scholarship of engagement. ASHE-ERIC Higher Education Report, 29*(5). San Francisco, CA: Jossey-Bass.

Wells, C. (2016a). Enduring influence and untapped potential: Advancing the conversation around scholarship reconsidered. In D. Moser, T. Read, & J. Braxton (Eds.), *Scholarship reconsidered: Expanded edition* (pp. 161–165). San Francisco, CA: Jossey-Bass.

Wells, C. (2016b). Realizing general education: Reconceptualizing purpose and renewing practice. *ASHE Higher Education Report, 42*(2). San Francisco, CA: Jossey-Bass.

Western Association of Schools and Colleges (2013). *Handbook of accreditation revised.* Retrieved from https://www.wascsenior.org/resources/handbook-accreditation-2013

Zayed, K. S. (2012). Reform in the general education movement: The case of Michigan State University, 1938–1952. *Journal of General Education*, *61*(2), 141–175.

CYNTHIA A. WELLS is associate professor of higher education and director of The Ernest L. Boyer Center at Messiah College.

NEW DIRECTIONS FOR HIGHER EDUCATION • DOI: 10.1002/he

6

In this chapter we call for immediate action to prepare more dynamic transdisciplinary professionals by leveraging the scholarship of practice. Transdisciplinary refers to contexts both inside and outside of the academy where today's doctoral students will work.

The Scholars We Need: Preparing Transdisciplinary Professionals by Leveraging the Scholarship of Practice

Melissa McDaniels, Erik Skogsberg

The need for individuals with the capacity and courage to solve societal problems is growing exponentially. As we write this chapter, members of our communities are asking what individuals and institutions can do to solve some of the most urgent problems facing society today. How can the children of Flint, Michigan have access to safe drinking water? How can the number of police shootings against unarmed people of color stop? Innovative approaches to problem solving are also needed in our academic disciplines, where different fields are emerging and the boundaries separating disciplines are dissolving. New technologies are opening more doors to understanding complex scientific phenomenon and paving the way for broader access to formerly buried documents and artifacts of interest to historians and humanists. Finally, college and university faculty in the United States—individuals primarily responsible for developing students with the ability to create and apply knowledge—are under tremendous pressure to continue providing high-quality intellectual training, improve the quality of undergraduate education, and take on administrative roles rarely imagined and trained for, and generally "do more with less."

It is these complex challenges that call for the preparation of a new generation of scholars, "triple-helix" workers (Thune, 2010), who are prepared for dynamic roles across a variety of contexts. Traditionally, the term *scholar* has been used to describe individuals who have terminal research degrees, are experts in their disciplines, and enjoy engaging in work where *ideas* and *knowledge* are currency. In the United States and elsewhere, individuals are prepared and certified by doctoral programs to engage in work that may

NEW DIRECTIONS FOR HIGHER EDUCATION, no. 178, Summer 2017 © 2017 Wiley Periodicals, Inc.
Published online in Wiley Online Library (wileyonlinelibrary.com) • DOI: 10.1002/he.20235

include, but is not limited to, research problem (and question) identification, utilization of existing literature to situate research questions, project design and implementation, collection and analysis of data, and the communication of research results to varied audiences (Austin & McDaniels, 2006a; Palmer, Teffeau, & Pirmann, 2009). Epistemic differences within and across disciplines will influence the specific form these scholarly activities take. Doctoral programs typically involve phases of coursework and independent research with satisfactory progress assessed through qualifying exams and completion of doctoral dissertations.

Over the past 25 years, stakeholders concerned about the ongoing quality of doctoral education have acknowledged that this approach to training is too narrow and possibly less effective than it should be in preparing the scholars to address 21st-century problems. Following Boyer's (1990) call to broaden the nature of scholarship for which faculty are rewarded, Austin and McDaniels (2006b) suggested that graduate programs train doctoral students not only in the scholarship of discovery, but also the scholarships of integration, application, and teaching. Graduate programs have begun investing resources (e.g., graduate career services staff, internship directors) to help students both gain experience outside of the academy and translate their discipline-specific training into a set of professional competencies and appreciations (American Association for the Advancement of Science [AAAS],2016a; Austin & McDaniels, 2006a; Blickley et al., 2012; Modern Languages Association, 2016), which they will be able to apply in a variety of leadership, administrative, and research roles. Federal agencies have funded doctoral training grants like the National Science Foundation's Integrative Graduate Education and Research Traineeship program (IGERT) to help scientists in training to "build[ing] on the foundations of their disciplinary knowledge with interdisciplinary training" (Technical Education Research Center, 2016). These and many other efforts (some of which we will highlight in this chapter) have started to help broaden the portfolio of skills and appreciations of doctoral recipients. All of these changes are being made in spite of the ubiquity of discipline-based department structures at colleges and universities in the United States and beyond. Ultimately, in order to fully realize the transformative potential of the innovations already mentioned, our institutions of higher education must restructure themselves in new and innovative ways.

In this chapter we call for administrators, faculty, and doctoral students to take immediate action to prepare more dynamic *transdisciplinary professionals* by leveraging the scholarship of practice. We use *transdisciplinary* to refer to contexts both inside and outside the academy within which today's doctoral students will work—settings that reveal some of the very real and seemingly intractable challenges we mentioned earlier in this chapter. By *professionals* we refer to individuals who, as a result of their training and credentials, work in roles that allow for a certain amount of autonomy, are rewarded based upon merit, require self-directed learning to ensure understanding and use of cutting-edge knowledge, and are often acknowledged in a national or international context (Metzger, 1987). Society needs transdisciplinary professionals ready to collaborate with individuals in other fields to "conceptualize across theoretical perspectives and multiple levels at the outset of their scientific experience" (Nash, 2008). This is in contrast to scholars who are able to participate in interdisciplinary collaborations where they operate from a "disciplinary-specific basis to address [a] common problem" or from multidisciplinary collaborations where scholars "work in parallel or sequentially from [a] disciplinary-specific base to address common problems" (Rosenfield, 1992, p. 1351).

A gap currently exists between the institutions where graduate students are trained and the contexts in which they will work as scholars. The majority of universities in the United States and elsewhere are granting discipline-specific degrees for students who receive training in discipline-specific academic units. They are being trained as disciplinary experts for roles in which they will need to solve transdisciplinary problems. Colleges and universities will need to address the organizational and financial barriers that comprise this gap. Rosenfield (1992), in her critique of efforts to train transdisciplinary scholars who could address public health concerns, noted that the "institutional and financial obstacles impeding the progression of knowledge and theory are far more stubborn than the conceptual ones" (p. 1355). Despite institutional barriers that still exist, we mirror the recommendations of scholars currently engaging in transdisciplinary work who acknowledge a set of individual competencies needed to perform skillfully in a transdisciplinary context. These competencies are cognitive, interpersonal, and intrapersonal in nature, and include, for example, the ability to promote meaning making and foster a common language among teams, tolerate uncertainty, build trust and broker partnerships, hire and mentor colleagues, handle ambiguity, and perform under conditions of uncertainty (Gray, 2008; Nash, 2008; Thune, 2010). These competencies will enable scholars to thrive in transdisciplinary contexts by helping them engage in myriad dynamic *professional practices*, those goal-directed activities in which they will engage within professional work settings (Polkinghorne, 2004). However, preparing graduate students with the foundational competencies to engage in a variety of professional practices is not enough; we also recommend introducing doctoral students to, and having them engage in, a type of reflection known as the *scholarship of practice*. The scholarship of practice is a type of research that aims to improve professional performance of individuals who implement that scholarship and build a knowledge base on efficacious professional practices to help institutional and societal leaders in the academy, industry, and the public sectors (Braxton, 2005). The dynamism of the contexts within which our doctoral students will be working will require a different type of scholar than was previously produced by our doctoral programs: one strongly anchored in the scholarship of practice.

For the remainder of this chapter, we will discuss ways in which this potential can be activated by *compelling awareness, inspiring application*, and *engaging in* the scholarship of practice. The strategies we outline in this chapter are practices that faculty and administrators can implement that will be more or less effective when introduced at different stages of the graduate student socialization process. The heuristic we will use to describe these stages of socialization was developed by Thornton and Nardi (1975) and built on by Weidman, Twale, and Stein (2001). The stages of this model are labeled as *anticipatory, formal, informal*, and *personal*. We will be putting the spotlight on answers to this question: How can experts in one discipline (e.g., plant biology or art history) utilize research from different disciplines (e.g., education, management, communications) to drive professional practices (e.g., team-leadership, teaching or mentoring, personnel evaluation, project management) across a variety of contexts? We will invite graduate students and faculty in the disciplines to understand, appreciate, and engage in this work, with the ultimate goal of expanding and transforming what disciplinary scholars believe is rigorous work in their own disciplines. We will end this chapter with an invitation and challenge to readers to take an additional step—to consider how advocates of the scholarship of practice can more fully integrate their own work into the knowledge traditions and practices of the disciplines themselves. We are urging our disciplinary colleagues to do the same in an effort to further leverage our collective theoretical and practical capacities to address the challenges we face together to re-create disciplines and institutions that will better address problems across our society.

Compelling Awareness of the Scholarship of Practice

In the early years of graduate study, students take courses and collaborate with their peers to refine their understanding of foundational literature and methodologies of a discipline. This intense focus can cause graduate students to become quickly immersed in—and take as sacrosanct—the traditions and epistemologies of fairly narrow fields of study, and the students are rewarded for doing so. This can result in students becoming embedded in, or having overly subjective relationships (Kegan, 2004) with, their own disciplines and epistemological stances. Regardless of their ultimate career path, it is important for doctoral students to develop the ability to engage in a set of professional practices and become aware that efficacious implementation of these practices relies upon an accessible scholarly knowledge base. In order to do this, they must emerge from this aforementioned embeddedness. Further, they must see their own disciplinary epistemologies objectively as only one of many legitimate knowledge sources and even as knowledge sources with limitations. This will enable doctoral students to be more open to the existence of legitimate professional practices and scholarship on topics they might have intuitively felt were important but perhaps viewed as "soft" or not as rigorous as ideas in their own fields. But awareness of the scholarship of practice won't happen by simply telling doctoral students that it exists. For example, Pizzolato's (2005) work with college students indicated that adults can be compelled to make this type of subject/object shift by experiencing *provocative moments,* some of which can be " … externally induced through programming, interventions and reforms" (p. 624) related to common academic experiences. It is essential we go beyond merely exposing doctoral students to this work. Instead, we must intentionally align policies and programming to engender moments and experiences that truly show the persuasive efficacy of the scholarship of practice and compel developing scholars toward application and future contribution to the scholarship of professional practice outside and inside their disciplines. If strategies are not compelling, doctoral students will not be motivated to sustain engagement in the scholarship of practice across their careers.

Compelling strategies best suited to the earlier *anticipatory* stages of socialization are those that gradually promote graduate student awareness of the cultural norms, beliefs and characteristics of the scholarship of practice. Strategies amenable to this stage of socialization include:

- *Communicating consistently the importance of professional competency development* starting during graduate student recruitment and continuing on through matriculation and the first year of doctoral study. Faculty can assure consistent messaging through doctoral program mission statements, recruitment materials, and program materials. Intentional communication of this type sends the message that these cross-field professional practices form the foundation of high-quality research and scholarly products. Departments can bring in program alumni, senior graduate students, and postdoctoral fellows to talk about what they wish they had known about important areas for professional development upon starting their own programs of study.
- Encouraging new doctoral students to regularly read articles and blogs about higher education and the academy. Faculty can also encourage graduate students to reach beyond disciplinary sources and read publications like the Chronicle of Higher Education and Inside Higher Education.

Compelling strategies best suited to the earlier *formal* stages of socialization are those in which faculty and administrators can provide groups of graduate students with structured educational experiences that further the professional socialization process. Some of these more formalized strategies include:

- *Assigning journal articles, blogs, or books that discuss scholarship related to different professional practices* whether in a pro-seminar or a journal club. Examples might include sources discussing such topics as efficacious teaching or mentoring practices in higher education or a particular discipline. These articles are ubiquitous and can be found in journals supported by disciplinary research societies (e.g., *Chemical Education, Clinical and Translational Science, The Journal of Higher Education*).
- *Creating workshops intended for a cross-departmental audiences of doctoral students on how to develop some of these key professional competencies.* Faculty can invite individuals with a deep knowledge of research supporting efficacious implementation of the practices in question. They can also be intentional about providing citations or resources to support recommendations and best practices discussed in these workshops.
- Including doctoral students in university-wide discussions about professional competencies and practices that are important for graduate students to develop. Faculty can make graduate students aware that these conversations are happening on campus and encourage them to participate in meetings. They can also share reports from different disciplinary societies, existing research on graduate student competency development, and guidelines from different professional societies that highlight the importance of certain competencies. Finally, faculty can identify the competencies that repeatedly appear in materials from each of these resources.

While recognizing the value of these strategies in promoting compelling awareness of the scholarship of practice, we urge our institutions to go further and create compelling conditions and experiences that inspire application of the scholarship of practice.

Inspiring Application of the Scholarship of Practice

Recently, many professional development opportunities have emerged and are supported by individual institutions, disciplinary societies, and agencies to urge doctoral students to begin to apply efficacious practices emerging from the literature. This application is an essential part of dynamically engaging with the scholarship of practice toward eventual contribution to that knowledge base. We find many doctoral students already have questions related to their own leadership, mentoring, teaching, and communication practices. They often do not trust their intuition to seek out answers and knowledge from other disciplines to answer those questions. Those of us directly involved in mentoring doctoral students need to affirm these instincts and help them develop courage and trust in pursuing answers—inspiring transdisciplinary application of the scholarship of practice toward potential solutions.

New Directions for Higher Education • DOI: 10.1002/he

None of the stages of socialization we referenced earlier in this chapter exists in a pure form in practice. As stages of doctoral study progress, formal socialization processes start to become integrated with informal socialization processes. Learning continues through exposure, observation, and conversations within structured groups of graduate students and faculty (Austin & McDaniels, 2006a). However, as time progresses, faculty and administrators can provide experiences that help graduate students recognize nuances of how scholars in a discipline inhabit that field by investing in smaller group experiences that will attract different subgroups of doctoral students. Examples of strategies particularly suited to the *informal* stages of socialization include:

- *Promoting access to cohort-based learning communities.* There are many examples of graduate schools that have created and sponsor cohort-based learning communities on professional practices related to leadership or teaching. A marked characteristic of these communities is, for example, requirements of reading the scholarly literature related to efficacious leadership or teaching practices. Cornell University's John and Jane Colman Family Endowed Fund for Leadership (http://gradschool.cornell.edu/leadership) and the University of California Santa Cruz's Graduate Student Leadership Certificate Program (http://graddiv.ucsc.edu/current-students/grad-student-resources/grad-student-leadership-prog.html) are both examples of learning communities aiming to develop a range of leadership skills. The Center for the Integration of Research, Teaching and Learning (CIRTL) Network (www.cirtl.net) supports a range of cohort-based teaching programs at universities across the country where students get exposure to the latest literature on effective teaching.
- *Providing support for students to attend pre-conference workshops on topics related to professional development.* The National Research Mentoring Network (https://nrmnet.net) offers a number of pre-conference workshops at disciplinary and professional society meetings (e.g., American Society for Microbiology) on the topic of research mentoring (National Institute of General Medical Sciences, 2016). The curriculum of these workshops is marked by both exposure to and practice with inclusive mentoring practices and exposure to the results of randomized control trials that have demonstrated the efficacy of the curriculum being presented.
- Inviting doctoral students to draft sections of federal grant applications that specifically ask for strategies to promote professional development for members of research teams in areas such as mentoring and communication to nonscientific audiences. This is particularly relevant for graduate students in both the social science and science, technology, engineering and math (STEM) disciplines.

Through application, doctoral students can develop the confidence and competence they will need to ultimately engage in scholarship of practice inside and outside their disciplines.

Engaging in the Scholarship of Practice

In this chapter we have challenged our readers to think about how to compel awareness among doctoral students in the disciplines about the importance of professional practices and about the existence of research literature, provide them with opportunities to interrogate research supporting professional practices, and experiment with implementing those practices. A smaller number of graduate students may be prepared to step into leadership roles that enrich conversations about the research and scholarship underpinning professional practices in which they are currently engaged as graduate students, employees, and/or community members. If faculty members and administrators provide doctoral students with opportunities not just to access and apply the scholarship of practice, but to add to the knowledge base, they will be giving graduate students the skills they will need to push boundaries of knowledge in their own disciplines and successfully engage in important transdisciplinary work in their future professional roles. Over the next several paragraphs, we highlight the strategies used by institutions and national networks that are investing in projects supporting student production of the scholarship of practice. These strategies are particularly effective and targeted for doctoral students entering the *personal* stage of socialization. Austin and McDaniels (2006a) assert that upon entering this phase of socialization, graduate students have more freedom to make decisions about the time they invest in developing themselves in professional areas including teaching, research, and leadership. They begin to move "towards being scholars and colleagues of established professionals in the field" (p. 403) with their own commitments and priorities.

Mentored Scholarship of Practice Projects. As doctoral students advance through their degree programs, they develop an increasingly refined ability to identify research problems, design research projects, collect data and communicate results. Once doctoral students reach the third or fourth years of their academic programs, some may be ready to apply these skills to scholarship of practice projects of their own. These projects are often marked by faculty member supervision as well as peer support from other doctoral students, often, but not always, in the form of learning communities. Professional learning communities are particularly effective in supporting student completion of such projects because of extended time periods for peer-to-peer feedback on different iterations of project design. Programs that exist to provide these project-based opportunities to doctoral students often start with, but do not need to rely upon, the support of financial resources from nationwide disciplinary and professional networks.

Examples of Scholarship of Practice Projects. The possibility exists for institutions to scaffold scholarship of practice projects in a variety of domains, including leadership, enrollment management, recruitment, and retention. However, most of the exemplars of institutional scaffolding of such projects relate to professional practices enacted in teaching roles.

Scholars and policy makers involved in STEM-education reform recommend that science should be taught with the same rigor as research is practiced (American Association for the Advancement of Science, 2016b). This community of reformers utilize the terms *teaching-as-research* (Center for the Integration of Teaching and Learning, 2016; Duckworth, 1986) and *scientific teaching* (Ebert-May, Hodder, Williams, & Luckie, 2004) to refer to the process of asking important questions about student learning outcomes, identifying data needed to answer those questions, developing the instruments to collect that data, and designing the curriculum that is aligned with achievement of those outcomes. We are suggesting that these terms and processes are examples of scholarship of professional teaching practice. Two examples of programs that support doctoral students in implementing scholarship of teaching practice projects exist at universities that are part of the CIRTL Network. In 2014, Claudia Vergara and others from Michigan State University described the nature of teaching-as-research projects implemented by participants of the Future Academic Scholars in Teaching (FAST) fellowship program:

> The development of TAR [teaching as research] projects is iterative. Typically, fellows begin with a research question, refine their research question and objectives, revisit their objectives to determine if they are measurable, develop their methods (data collection and analyses), and then prepare their data interpretation and results. Finally, fellows address how they will use their results to inform teaching and learning. The scheme mirrors the way in which graduate students regularly present their research progress in disciplinary research group meetings. (p. 97)

At Cornell University, experienced graduate instructors undertake small-scale classroom research projects as a part of Cornell's Scholarship of Teaching and Learning Practitioner Program, receiving

> ... training and support needed to conduct a small-scale classroom research project and present the results in a poster session to the campus community... have [ing] the opportunity to develop a manuscript ... and ... become a part of a larger cohort of fellows serving as campus-wide leaders in advancing teaching excellence. (Cornell University, 2016)

Once graduate students start to understand and produce the scholarship of practice based in the research of other disciplines, they may also

NEW DIRECTIONS FOR HIGHER EDUCATION • DOI: 10.1002/he

come to re-create what is researchable and important in their own discipline and in the scholarship of practice.

Re-Creating the Scholarship of Practice

Compelling awareness, inspiring application, and engaging in the scholarship of practice has the potential to empower students to utilize empirical and/or theoretical evidence instead of relying upon "common sense" or "management fads" (Birnbaum, 2000) as they enact professional practices while in their graduate training programs and over the course of their careers. It is also true that this process will be uncomfortable for some; it will require doctoral students to embrace a novice identity as they learn about the scholarship that exists on their work practices while at the same time strengthening their identities as experts.

Colleges and universities have already benefitted from the infusion of the scholarship of practice work, especially as it relates to teaching practice. Doctoral-granting institutions often rely on graduate teaching assistants to instruct many undergraduate courses. Some of these institutions, with support of the National Science Foundation, the Council of Graduate Schools, the Teagle and Sloan Foundations (among others), have created opportunities for graduate students to use evidence-based research to empower them to more effectively assess and improve undergraduate student learning. In this chapter, we suggest different strategies that faculty and administrators may find effective in supporting individuals at different stages of the graduate school socialization process.

Concluding Thoughts

As we conclude this chapter, we urge readers to consider the potential for the scholarship of practice not just to improve practice, but to re-create the institutions and disciplines that still play a powerful role in both promoting and limiting the potential of doctoral education programs. We are hoping the experiences some doctoral students will have producing the scholarship of practice will contribute, over the course of their careers, to the re-creation of what their fields are and could be. As we stated earlier, the challenges facing society, the scientific enterprise and our postsecondary institutions are already destabilizing how our scholars are trained in the early years of this century. In higher education, new transdisciplinary doctoral programs are being designed and assessed. Institutions, disciplinary societies, and professional associations are reconsidering what the nature and format of the doctoral dissertation should be. Doctoral students, after participating in programs in which they produced the scholarship of practice, are returning to their disciplines, partnering with willing faculty to engage in research that challenges the norms of mentoring, research, and teaching practices in their own fields, and further embedding some of these research results

NEW DIRECTIONS FOR HIGHER EDUCATION • DOI: 10.1002/he

in discipline-based outlets. Doctoral students are starting to occupy spaces within their disciplinary research communities where the challenges to traditional paradigms and practices are themselves being questioned. These and other seemingly small steps will play a role in preparing scholars who are professionals able to skillfully navigate transdisciplinary contexts that require the openness and creativity required for new approaches to old and new problems inside and outside the academy.

Given the time pressures facing faculty and doctoral students, this chapter raises some important practical issues, including how doctoral students, as evolving experts in discipline-specific doctoral programs, can have the time and develop the skills to access and utilize empirical research from scholars in other disciplines to prepare them to engage in efficacious professional practices. A small number of transdisciplinary doctoral programs and departments now exist, and it remains to be seen if these structures and related investments continue.

In this chapter, we built upon Braxton's (2005) goals for the scholarship of practice and argue that engaging doctoral students in the scholarship of practice will make them more dynamic: scholars not only open to other epistemologies but also motivated by the possibility of collaborating with colleagues in other disciplines to transcend embedded disciplinary traditions and re-create new models that mark transdisciplinary work. This new crop of transdisciplinary professionals would be prepared to dynamically and flexibly collaborate with others to respond to the challenges and opportunities presented by imminent questions emerging across our communities, disciplines, and institutions.

References

American Association for the Advancement of Science (AAAS). (2016a). *My IDP*. Retrieved from http://myidp.sciencecareers.org/

American Association for the Advancement of Science (AAAS). (2016b). *Communicating science workshops*. Center for Public Engagement with Science and Technology. Retrieved from http://www.aaas.org/pes/communicating-science-workshops

Austin, A. E., & McDaniels, M. (2006a). Preparing the professoriate of the future: Graduate student socialization for faculty roles. In J. C. Smart (Ed.), *Higher education: Handbook of theory and research*, *11*, 397–456.

Austin, A. E., & McDaniels, M. (2006b). Using doctoral education to prepare faculty to work within Boyer's four domains of scholarship. In J. M. Braxton (Ed.), *New Directions for Institutional Research: No. 129. Analyzing faculty work and rewards: Using Boyer's four domains of scholarship* (pp. 51–65). San Francisco, CA: Jossey-Bass.

Birnbaum, R. (2000). *Management fads in higher education: Where they come from, what they do, and why they fail*. San Francisco, CA: Jossey-Bass.

Blickley, J. L., Deiner, K., Garbach, K., Lacher, I., Meek, M. H., Porensky, L. M., ... Schwartz, M. W. (2013). Graduate student's guide to necessary skills for nonacademic conservation careers. *Conservation Biology*, *27*, 24–34. https://doi.org/10.1111/j.1523-1739.2012.01956.x

Boyer, E. L. (1990). *Scholarship reconsidered: Priorities of the professoriate*. San Francisco, CA: Jossey-Bass.

Braxton, J. M. (2005). Reflections on a scholarship of practice. *The Review of Higher Education*, 28(2), 285–293.

Center for the Integration of Research, Teaching and Learning. (2016). Teaching-as-research. Retrieved from https://www.cirtl.net/p/core-ideas-teaching-as-research

Cornell University. (2016). *Scholarship of teaching and learning practitioner program*. Cornell University Graduate School. Retrieved from http://gradschool.cornell.edu/cu-cirtl/SOTL-program

Duckworth, E. (1986). Teaching as research. *Harvard Educational Review*, 56(4), 481–496.

Ebert-May, D., Hodder, J., Williams, K., & Luckie, D. (2004). Pathways to scientific teaching. *Frontiers in Ecology and the Environment*, 2(6), 1–323. Retrieved from http://www.jstor.org/stable/3868408

Gray, B. (2008). Enhancing transdisciplinary research through collaborative leadership. *American Journal of Preventative Medicine*, 35(2S), S124–S132.

Kegan, R. (2004). *In over our heads: The mental demands of modern life*. Cambridge, MA: Harvard University Press.

Metzger, W. P. (1987). The academic profession in the United States. In B. Clark (Ed.), *The academic profession: National, disciplinary and institutional settings*. Berkeley, CA: University of California Press.

Modern Languages Association. (2016). Preparing for life outside the academy: A primer and resource guide. Retrieved from https://www.mla.org/Resources/Career/Career-Resources

Nash, J. M. (2008). Transdisciplinary training: Key components and prerequisites for success. *American Journal of Preventative Medicine*, 35(2S), S133–S140.

National Institute of General Medical Sciences. (2016). *The National Research Mentoring Network (NRMN)*. Retrieved from https://www.nigms.nih.gov/training/dpc/pages/nrmn.aspx

Palmer, C. L., Teffeau, L. C., & Pirmann, C. M. (2009). *Scholarly information practices in the online environment: Themes from the literature and implications for library service development*. Dublin, OH: OCLC Research. Retrieved from http://www.oclc.org/research/publications/library/2009/2009-02.pdf

Pizzolato, J. E. (2005). Creating crossroads for self-authorship: Investigating the provocative moment. *Journal of College Student Development*, 46(6), 624–641.

Polkinghorne, D. (2004). *Practice and the human sciences: The case for a judgement-based practice of care*. Albany: State University of New York Press.

Rosenfield, P. L. (1992). The potential of transdisciplinary research for sustaining and extending linkages between the health and social sciences. *Social Science & Medicine*, 35(11), 1343–1357.

Technical Education Resource Center. (2016). *About IGERT*. Retrieved November 27, 2016 from http://www.igert.org/public/about

Thornton, R., & Nardi, P. M. (1975). The dynamics of role acquisition. *American Journal of Sociology*, 80(4), 870–885.

Thune, T. (2010). The training of "triple-helix workers"? Doctoral students in university-industry-government collaborations. *Minerva*, 48, 463–483.

Vergara, C. E., Urban-Lurain, M., Campa, H., Cheruvelil, K. S., Ebert-May, D., Fata-Hartley, C., & Johnston, K. (2014). FAST (Future Academic Scholars in Teaching): A high-engagement development program for future STEM faculty. *Innovative Higher Education*, 39(2), 93–107.

Weidman, J.C., Twale, D.J., & Stein, E.L. (2001). Socialization of graduate and professional students in higher education—A perilous passage? *ASHE-ERIC Higher Education Report*, 28(3). Washington, DC: The George Washington University, School of Education and Human Development.

MELISSA MCDANIELS is Assistant Dean of the Graduate School at Michigan State University. She is also the co-director of the Master Facilitator Initiative through the NIH-supported National Research Mentoring Network (NIH # - U54GM119023)

ERIK SKOGSBERG is a Teacher Learning Designer in the Hub for Innovation in Learning and Technology and a PhD candidate in Curriculum, Instruction, and Teacher Education (CITE) at Michigan State University.

(ACPA/NASPA, 2015, p. 11). Finally, in professional preparation academic programs, faculty members can integrate the competency areas into specific course learning outcomes, use them to inform their research agendas, and guide their ongoing professional development.

Graduate Preparation Programs. Entry to full-time employment in the field of student affairs typically requires the credential of a master's degree. Student affairs master's level graduate preparation program curricula are often guided by the CAS standards, whereas some counselor educator programs with a specialty area in college counseling and student affairs are accredited by the Council for Accreditation of Counseling and Related Educational Programs. Although the curricular requirements of these two organizations differ, areas of overlap include an emphasis on students developing the knowledge of foundational theories, the skills to apply them to practice, and the use of multiple data sources to inform programs and services that solve problems in higher education settings. Finally, to provide apprenticeship opportunities for the application of theory in professional settings alongside established mentors, the curricula of both types of programs require students to complete internships (Council for the Advancement of Standards in Higher Education, 2015; Council for the Accreditation of Counseling and Related Educational Programs, 2016).

Professional Associations. Currently, dozens of student affairs-related professional associations exist, including two large, generalist student affairs professional associations: ACPA and NASPA. Many others focus on a particular, specialized functional area such as housing, orientation, academic advising, fraternity and sorority life, or financial aid.

Professional associations reinforce the scholarship of practice by providing structure and opportunities for the generation and dissemination of knowledge sources too numerous to catalog, but we highlight some of the ways they promote the scholarship of practice. These associations sponsor the development and exchange of scholarship through funding research grants, providing writing awards, encouraging research paper presentations and poster sessions at professional meetings, and publishing scholarly work in journals, books, and other media. Also, student affairs-related publications examine the process of how theory can and should inform professional practice (see Blimling, 2011; Patton, Renn, Guido, & Quaye, 2016; Reason & Kimball, 2012). A second way professional associations support the value of integrating scholarship with practice is to require conference presenters to identify appropriate theoretical frameworks and provide research evidence in scholarly paper proposals. Similarly, rubric criteria for writing and excellence awards often include application of research, theory, or assessment. In exchange for accessing its membership for survey research, some associations expect researchers to report the findings and implications of the study to the membership in the form of a conference program or publication.

Another way professional association leaders promote the scholarship of practice is by fostering meaningful interactions among practitioners and faculty. Graduate preparation faculty members partner with professional associations in student affairs by serving as officers, committee and task-force members, and leaders in other varied roles. ACPA's Commission for Professional Preparation, ACPA's Emerging and Senior Scholars, and NASPA's Faculty Council and Faculty Assembly, all serve as bodies that recognize and represent faculty in the associations. To foster connections with faculty and other researchers, the Association of College and University Housing Officers-International (ACUHO-I) sponsors both a funded research grant program and a larger multi-institutional research grant designed to investigate larger questions related to the field. Additionally, they have added "Just in Time" symposia to their educational portfolio, which are programs designed to quickly respond to the educational needs of members who work in a mercurial environment. In a recent Just in Time initiative, ACUHO-I partnered housing practitioners with authors of the most recent edition of *How College Affects Students: 21st Century Evidence that Higher Education Works* (Mayhew et al., 2016), the third volume of a series that synthesizes research on college impact. The purpose of the day-and-a-half symposium was to focus on the findings related to students who live on campus and then consider ways the research could apply to practitioners' campuses using theory-to-practice process models. Finally, participants recommended future research areas that ACUHO-I should explore (Association of College and University Housing Officers-International, 2016).

Integrating the Scholarship of Practice: Strategies From Social Work

Examining how other professions integrate scholarship into practice can provide new insights into strategies to integrate the scholarship of practice. Accordingly, we consider the field of social work. Both education and social work have been classified as social and creative professions (Chynoweth, 2008), sharing characteristics of applied, nonparadigmatic (or soft) fields (Biglan, 1973). Professionals in applied fields tend to be more concerned with the ways in which knowledge can be useful in practice than are professionals in pure fields, such as physics or philosophy. Highly paradigmatic (or hard) fields share a consistent body of theory that is subscribed to by all members (Kuhn, 1962). In soft fields, there is less agreement on the problems and methods of inquiry of the discipline, compared with hard fields, such as chemistry or engineering (Biglan, 1973).

We highlight four key approaches that social work leaders employ to promote the use of evidence-based practice. First, the National Association of Social Workers (NASW) and the Council on Social Work Education (CSWE) share multiple website resources with members so that social work students and professionals can easily access current research findings related to their work. One resource for such practices is the Substance Abuse and Mental Health Services Administration federal agency (2016), which coordinates the National Registry of Evidence-Based Programs and Practices (NREPP). The purpose of the NREPP initiative is to promote the use of scientifically established behavioral health interventions to practitioners and the public. Over 350 substance-abuse and mental-health interventions are rated based on six criteria. Second, CSWE encourages social work faculty members to incorporate evidence-based practice and evidence-supported treatments into their courses. CSWE collects and publishes model syllabi that demonstrate various ways that colleagues address these topics in social work academic preparation programs (CSWE, 2016). Third, the CSWE's (2015) Educational Policy and Accreditation Standards for Baccalaureate and Master's Social Work Programs were approved by both the Commission on Accreditation and the Commission on Educational Policy. Of nine outlined competencies necessary for successful practice, nearly all mention assessing outcomes, applying theory, or using research evidence to inform practice or policy. Two specifically relate to the scholarship of practice. Finally, several social work institutes publish Internet-accessible evidence–based mapping interventions; manual-guided, evidence-supported treatment plans; and policy recommendations (see Institute of Behavioral Research, 2016 and the Social Work Policy Institute, 2016a, 2016b). It should be noted that the emphasis on evidence-based practice has its critics. Some social workers are concerned that the evidence-supported treatments may not adequately address the needs of diverse populations and that not all practitioners may be trained to implement them competently (Barth et al., 2012).

Recommendations

Integrating the scholarship of practice is a core value of student affairs educators, yet potential exists for improvement. Essential knowledge in student affairs is intellectual curiosity and the "capacity to continually reflect on the intersections of knowledge and action" (Baxter Magolda & Magolda, 2011, p. 5). The ability to access, integrate, and apply multiple sources of knowledge is key to successful student affairs practice. Thus, we offer the following recommendations:

   Access.   We recommend three strategies to increase access to existing research findings related to college students. Acknowledging that the student affairs field is multidisciplinary, the knowledge base could benefit from systematically compiling research findings about college students and postsecondary education from other disciplines (e.g., psychology, sociology, cultural studies, political science). Second, the Institute of Education Sciences' What Works Clearinghouse (WWC, 2016) offers a summary report of high quality research on various education interventions. The purpose of the WWC is to provide educational practitioners with an objective, rigorous review so they can make evidence-based decisions. In 2016, the WWC published postsecondary-related intervention reports that address outcomes of ACT/SAT test preparation and coaching programs, first-year experience courses, developmental education, and summer-bridge programs. Third, editors of professional journals and doctoral dissertation advisors could investigate the criteria for a study's inclusion in the WWC systematic review of research. If the criteria were more closely aligned, additional student affairs research studies would then be included.

Integrate. A mechanism designed to summarize research findings and publish research briefs on relevant topics for practitioner audiences may encourage more integration of empirically based research in practice. Professional associations could feature such briefs on their websites as a resource for members. Second, student affairs supervisors could require that proposals for funding new projects provide supportive empirical evidence and/or require rigorous evaluations for continued funding and resources. Third, professional preparation faculty can adjust course assignments to enhance students' knowledge and skills related to finding and evaluating empirical evidence.

Apply. Professional development opportunities to learn techniques of applying scholarship to practice could support professionals in progressing from foundational to intermediate and advanced competency levels. Student case-study competitions could require that participants support recommended actions with theory and or empirically based research. Finally, partnerships among professional associations bring coherence to the field's identity and professional standards. Similar collaborations to deepen the knowledge base and communicate the findings to both internal and external audiences may more effectively inform campus colleagues, the general public, and policy makers of the role and contributions of student affairs educators.

Conclusion

Although the student affairs profession adapts to constant change, characteristics of the roles of the early deans that were shaped by the "resources devoted to the program by the institution's administration, the urban or nonurban setting of the campus, and the composition of the student body" (Williamson & Darley, 1937, p. 47) still ring true with contemporary professionals. Fortunately, student affairs educators now benefit from the support of professional associations, graduate preparation programs, a coherent set of professional standards, and a body of knowledge that informs professional practice. Intentional, collaborative efforts to expand the knowledge base and communicate theories and research findings in accessible ways for practitioners to inform their work will further foster the scholarship of practice and advance "deeper and more inclusive" practices and ideas (Dewey, 1938, p. v) in student affairs work.

References

American Association of Higher Education/American College Personnel Association/National Association of Student Personnel Administrators. (1998). *Powerful partnerships: A shared responsibility for learning.* Washington, DC: Authors.

American College Personnel Association. (1994). *The student learning imperative: Implications for student affairs.* Washington, DC: Author.

American College Personnel Association/National Association of Student Personnel Administrators. (2004). *Learning reconsidered: A campus-wide focus on the student experience.* Washington, DC: Authors.

American College Personnel Association/National Association of Student Personnel Administrators. (2015). *Professional competency areas for student affairs educators.* Washington, DC: Authors.

American College Personnel Association/Association of College and University Housing Officers-International/Association of College Unions-International/National Association for Campus Activities/National Academic Advising Association/National Association of Student Personnel Administrators/National Intramural Recreational Sports Association. (2006). *Learning reconsidered 2: Implementing a campus-wide focus on the student experience.* Washington, DC: Authors.

American Council on Education. (1937/1949). *The student personnel point of view.* Washington, DC: Author.

Association of College and University Housing Officers-International. (2016). *Just in time.* Columbus, OH: Authors. Retrieved from http://www.acuho-i.org/educational-events/just-in-time

Barth, R. P., Lee, B. R., Lindsey, M. A., Collins, K. S., Strieder, F., Chorpita, B. F., . . . Sparks, J. A. (2012). Evidence-based practice at a crossroads: The timely emergence of common elements and common factors. *Research on Social Work Practice, 22,* 108–119.

Baxter Magolda, M. B., & Magolda, P. M. (2011). What counts as "essential" knowledge for student affairs educators? In P. M. Magolda & M. B. Baxter Magolda (Eds.), *Contested issues in student affairs: Diverse perspectives and respectful dialogue* (pp. 3–14). Sterling, VA: Stylus.

Biglan, A. (1973). The characteristics of subject matters in different academic areas. *Journal of Applied Psychology, 57*(3), 195–203.

Blimling, G. S. (2011). How are dichotomies such as scholar/practitioner and theory/practice helpful and harmful to the profession? Developing professional judgment. In P. M. Magolda & M. B. Baxter Magolda (Eds.), *Contested issues in student affairs: Diverse perspectives and respectful dialogue* (pp. 42–53). Sterling, VA: Stylus.

Boyer, E. L. (1990). *Scholarship reconsidered: Priorities of the professoriate.* San Francisco, CA: Jossey-Bass.

Braxton, J. M. (2005). Reflections on a scholarship of practice. *The Review of Higher Education, 28,* 285–293.

Chynoweth, P. (2008). Legal research. In A. Knight & L. Ruddock (Eds.), *Advanced research methods in the built environment* (pp. 28–38). Oxford, UK: Wiley-Blackwell.

Coomes, M. D., & Gerda, J. J. (2015). A long and honorable history: Student affairs in the United States. In G. S. McClellan, J. Stringer, & Associates (Eds.), *The handbook of student affairs administration* (4th ed., pp. 2–24). San Francisco, CA: Jossey-Bass.

Council for Accreditation of Counseling & Related Educational Programs. (2016). *Section 5: Entry-Level specialty areas—college counseling and student affairs.* Alexandria, VA: Author. Retrieved from http://www.cacrep.org/section-5-entry-level-specialty-areas-college-counseling-and-student-affairs/

Council for the Advancement of Standards in Higher Education. (2015). *CAS professional standards for higher education* (9th ed.). Washington, DC: Author.

Council on Social Work Education. (2015). *Educational policy and accreditation standards for baccalaureate and master's social work programs*. Alexandria, VA: Author. Retrieved from http://www.cswe.org/File.aspx?id=81660

Council on Social Work Education. (2016). *Model EBP and EST syllabi*. Alexandria, VA: Author. Retrieved from http://www.cswe.org/CentersInitiatives/Curriculum Resources/TeachingEvidence-BasedPractice/ModelEBPandESTSyllabi.aspx

Dewey, J. (1938). *Experience in education*. New York, NY: Macmillan.

Institute of Behavioral Research. (2016). *Background and overview*. Fort Worth, TX: Texas Christian University. Retrieved from https://ibr.tcu.edu/manuals/background-and-overview/

Institute of Education Sciences, What Works Clearinghouse. (2016). *Find what works based on the evidence*. Washington, DC: Author. Retrieved from http://ies.ed.gov/ncee/wwc/FWW/Results?filters=,Postsecondary

Kuhn, T. S. (1962). *The structure of scientific revolutions*. Chicago, IL: University of Chicago Press.

Liddell, D. L., Wilson, M. E., Pasquesi, K., Hirschy, A. S, & Boyle, K. M. (2014). Development of professional identity through socialization in graduate school. *Journal of Student Affairs Research and Practice, 51*, 69–84.

Mayhew, M. J., Rockenbach, A. N., Bowman, N. A., Seifert, T. A., & Wolniak, G. C., with Pascarella, E. T., & Terenzini, P. T. (2016). *How college affects students (Vol. 3): 21st century evidence that higher education works*. San Francisco, CA: Jossey-Bass.

Patton, L. D., Renn, K. A., Guido, F. M. & Quaye, S. J. (2016). *Student development in college: Theory, research, and practice* (3rd ed.). San Francisco, CA: Jossey-Bass.

Reason, R. D., & Kimball, E. W. (2012). A new theory-to-practice model for student affairs: Integrating scholarship, context, and reflection. *Journal of Student Affairs Research and Practice, 49*, 359–376.

Rhatigan, J. J. (2009). From the people up: A brief history of student affairs administration. In G. S. McClellan, J. Stringer, & Associates (Eds.), *The handbook of student affairs administration* (3rd ed., pp. 3–18). San Francisco, CA: Jossey-Bass.

Social Work Policy Institute. (2016a). *Publications*. Washington, DC: Author. Retrieved from http://www.socialworkpolicy.org/publications.

Social Work Policy Institute. (2016b). *Evidence-based practice*. Washington, DC: Author. Retrieved from http://www.socialworkpolicy.org/research/evidence-based-practice-2.html.

Substance Abuse and Mental Health Services Administration. (2016). *National registry of evidence-based programs and practices*. Rockville, MD: Author. Retrieved by http://www.samhsa.gov/nrepp

Williamson, E. G., & Darley, J. G. (1937). *Student personnel work: An outline of clinical procedures*. New York, NY: McGraw-Hill.

Wilson, M. E., Liddell, D. L., Hirschy, A. S., & Pasquesi, K. (2016). Professional identity, career commitment, and career entrenchment of midlevel student affairs professionals. *Journal of College Student Development, 57*, 557–572.

Amy S. Hirschy is assistant professor in the College of Education and Human Development at the University of Louisville. She was an academic fellow for the Institute for Higher Education Policy.

Maureen E. Wilson is professor and chair of the Department of Higher Education and Student Affairs at Bowling Green State University. She is a senior scholar with ACPA: College Student Educators International.

8

This chapter describes the enactment of three levels of a scholarship of practice for higher education. The stewardship played by each of these levels constitutes the central focus of this chapter.

The Scholarship of Practice and Stewardship of Higher Education

John M. Braxton, Todd C. Ream

Through engagement in the scholarship of practice, scholars of higher education and practitioners in individual colleges and universities act as stewards of higher education. Engagement in the scholarship of practice vouchsafes that administrative practice, policy making, and other institutional actions find some basis in empirical research. Grounding such institutional matters in empirical research prevents colleges and universities from commonsensical "shooting from the hip" or "trial-and-error" forms of institutional action. Accordingly, engagement in the scholarship of practice constitutes an act of stewardship as it safeguards the welfare of higher education at the level of a social institution and at the level of the individual college or university.

This stewardship role manifests itself in different ways across the three levels of the scholarship of practice described by Kramer and Braxton in Chapter 1 of this volume. We describe these ways in subsequent sections of this chapter.

Level One of a Scholarship of Practice

In Chapter 1, Kramer and Braxton posit that Level One of a scholarship of practice entails the use of empirical research findings as a foundation for the development of institutional policy and practice. Institutional practitioners who use empirical research as a foundation for the development of policy and practice at their college or university function as stewards of the institution's welfare. Herein, we assert that theoretically grounded research findings can shape the development of institutional policies and practices. The use of theory-based research contributes to an understanding of the underlying basis of the recommendations formulated, and such understanding leads to the reliable implementation of the focal recommendation and

NEW DIRECTIONS FOR HIGHER EDUCATION, no. 178, Summer 2017 © 2017 Wiley Periodicals, Inc.
Published online in Wiley Online Library (wileyonlinelibrary.com) • DOI: 10.1002/he.20237

provides a basis for adjustments or changes (Braxton et al., 2014). However, we realize not all research pertinent to practice is guided by theory. In such instances, the use of findings of empirical research suffices. By using empirical research as a basis for the formulation of institutional policy and action, practitioners prevent their institution from otherwise ill-informed types of decision-making and intuitional action.

Such stewardship at its highest level occurs when members of the central administration of a college or university, such as the president and/or chief academic affairs officer, use empirical research findings to guide their development of institutional policy and other forms of institutional action and decision-making. Other institutional practitioners might also participate in this form of the scholarship of practice and act as stewards of the institution's well being. These individuals include faculty members involved in institutional governance, chief student-affairs officers, institutional-advancement officers, admissions officers, and staff members in domains of student affairs such as academic advisement, residential life, student orientation, fraternity and sorority advisement, and student activities.

Jillian Kinzie in Chapter 4 describes ways in which colleges and universities that participated in the National Survey of Student Engagement (NSSE) use findings from their administration of the NSSE. Her examples give clarity to how empirical research findings can be used to inform institutional practice. For its most recent reaccreditation review with the Middle States Commission on Higher Education, a liberal arts college used NSSE results to offer evidence of improved student learning through its systematic use of indirect assessments. Kinzie also discusses how one university used NSSE measures to assess the extent to which students experienced cultural diversity. She notes the findings of this assessment were used to warrant the university's decision to modify its diversity requirements as part of the general education component of the university's curriculum.

For individual practitioners seeking guidance on the process of translating research findings into policy and practice, Wilson and Hirschy in Chapter 3 describe two models designed for this purpose: the Model of Theory-to-Practice Translation (Reason & Kimball, 2012) and the Action Inquiry Model (St. John, McKinney, & Tuttle, 2006). Wilson and Hirschy also offer recommendations for selecting theoretically derived models. Beyond guidance on the process of translating research findings into a form amenable for institutional policy and practice, Wilson and Hirschy also offer recommendations on how an institutional practitioner can identify problems that may benefit from the application of empirical research for their resolution.

As Hirschy and Wilson state in Chapter 7, individual practitioners of higher education best equipped to engage in Level One of the scholarship of practice are graduates of masters and doctoral programs in higher education as a field of study in general and of student affairs preparation programs in particular. However, doctoral programs in higher education as a field of study should work toward the preparation of scholars of professional practice by including relevant topics in courses, in questions on doctoral qualifying examinations, and in guidance for dissertation work (Braxton, 2005). Student affairs graduate preparation programs provide a model for stressing the importance of infusing theory and empirically based research into professional practice. Hirschy and Wilson describe ways student affairs preparation programs work toward inculcating the importance of the use of both theory and empirical research to guide administrative practice.

Although Level One of a scholarship of practice for higher education focuses on the use of empirical research findings to address policy and practice at the individual college or university level, we also posit herein that institutional leaders and scholars of higher education might use empirical research findings to shed light on issues facing the lay public. Put differently, institutional practitioners or scholars of higher education might also play the role of public intellectuals who function as stewards of higher education at the level of a social institution. Acts of public intellectualism potentially demonstrate the need for higher education as a public good.

Public Intellectuals and the Scholarship of Practice.   A brief discussion of the public intellectual will offer aspiring scholars of practice some points of inspiration from the historically honored identity of the public intellectual. Scholars of practice and public intellectuals undoubtedly have some differences in terms of how they view their identity and work. Regardless, they share an enormous amount of "requisite perspective, temperament, character, and knowledge" (Posner, 2001, p. 9). In fact, they share far more in common than what otherwise might divide them. As a result, aspiring scholars of practice can learn a considerable amount from individuals who formally or informally embraced the mantle of public intellectual.

In his book *Public Intellectuals: A Study in Decline* (2001), Richard Posner, a judge on the United States Court of Appeals for the Seventh Circuit, explores the decline in the number of public intellectuals. His concerns parallel our concerns about the need for more scholars of practice in academe. Posner offers what proves to be a helpful assessment of the role of the public intellectual as a "critical commentator addressing a nonspecialist audience on matters of broad public concern" (p. 9). The one obvious difference between the public intellectual and the scholar of practice is the context from which their commentaries emerge. In particular, while the public intellectual in Posner's sense is a "critical commentator," the commentary of the scholar of practice often emerges through practical attempts to address a challenge of concern to a particular public. For higher education scholars, that public, as we have discussed, is often their own respective college or university. Admittedly risking oversimplification, the public intellectual is more of a theorist and the scholar of practice is more of a practitioner.

Despite that subtle yet significant difference, another set of factors that the scholar of practice and the public intellectual share comes through in the challenges they face. In particular, Posner notes that the decline in the work of the public intellectual is directly related to "the rise of the modern university and the concomitant trend toward an even greater specialization of knowledge" (pp. 3–4).

Posner (2001) is quick to note that specialization is not bad in and of itself, and thus, in many cases the outcomes of such a focus are positive. However, when allowed to become a totalizing focus, the depth of knowledge that specialization enables is purchased at the expense of breadth, while the working conditions of the modern university, in particular, the principle of academic freedom backed by the tenure contract, make the intellectual's career a safe, comfortable one, which can breed aloofness and complexity.

The public intellectual, as well as the scholar of practice, deals with questions that all too often transcend disciplinary and sub-disciplinary boundaries. In order to do their work, they must reach across divides rarely traversed and do so, according to Posner (2001), in a manner that is counter-intuitive to the present logic of the modern university.

The globalized nature of higher education has also compelled scholars to consider how geographical and cultural particularity impact how public intellectuals conceive of and practice their work. Two examples of these types of works include Romila Thapar's *The Public Intellectual in India* (2015) and Nelson Wiseman's *The Public Intellectual in Canada* (2013). Such volumes reinforce that while the globalized context in which there are public intellectuals is growing, regional differences still matter in relation to the work they do and the audiences they serve. Like public intellectuals, scholars of practice may engage with the lay public of their local communities or state.

Perhaps the works most relevant to our specific conversation are discipline-specific offerings. For example, Charles Gattone's, *The Social Scientist as Public Intellectual: Critical Reflections in a Changing World* (2006) has ramifications for how higher education scholars might think about their work. Although not specifically addressing higher education scholars as public intellectuals, Mary Beth Gasman's recent edited volume, *Academics Going Public: How to Write and Speak Beyond Academe* (2016), introduces higher education scholars to many of the sensibilities and practices of the public intellectual. We recommend these works to those scholars of practice desiring more information about the role of the public intellectual.

Level Two of the Scholarship of Practice

In Chapter 1 of this volume, Kramer and Braxton define Level Two as empirical research directed toward the acquisition of three forms of professional knowledge described by Eraut (1988): replicative, applicatory, and interpretative. Eraut defines replicative knowledge as a familiarity with the requisite routines and interactions of the role of a professional, applicatory knowledge as entailing the conversion of technical knowledge into plans for action, and interpretative knowledge as knowledge rooted in wisdom and judgment on the part of the user. Scholars of higher education participate in Level Two of the scholarship of practice by first conducting research and scholarship designed to contribute to one of these three forms of professional knowledge and then through publishing articles in journals of higher education.

Stewardship assumes a different form for Level Two. As the articles published contribute to the three forms of professional knowledge, they also constitute acts of stewardship toward the welfare of these forms. Such publications also function as stewards of administrative practice for individual institutions by moving administrative practice beyond otherwise speculative means of decision-making and action. In a larger sense, higher education as a social institution also benefits from Level Two scholarship of practice.

Scholars of higher education as a field of study and scholars from other academic disciplines wishing to engage in scholarship that produces replicative, applicatory, and interpretative forms of professional knowledge may be unfamiliar with the administrative work in higher education needed to produce such knowledge. To help ease that challenge, Lyken-Segosebe in Chapter 2 provides a good starting place. She points to the scholarship of practice produced by such fields of study as pharmacy, nursing, and occupational therapy as exemplars of how a scholarship of practice develops. She states that practice scholarship in these three fields use "a knowledge of practice to generate knowledge for practice."

A knowledge of practice is important to research and scholarship needed to generate replicative, applicatory, and interpretative forms of professional knowledge. Some guidance on developing a knowledge of practice exists in the literature (Braxton, 2005). For example, the development of replicative knowledge requires a knowledge of the "routines" of different forms of administrative work (Eraut, 1988) such as the presidency, academic affairs administration, student affairs administration, admissions, and institutional advancement. Braxton (2005) posits that the empirical delineation of administrative routines constitutes an initial step that can be followed by empirical studies of the performance of these routines of administrative work. For instance, faculty hiring decisions and faculty personnel decisions such as reappointment, tenure, and promotion constitute examples of routine practices of academic administrative work (Braxton, 2005).

The development of applicatory professional knowledge centers attention on the translation of technical knowledge into action (Eraut, 1988). For example, the dynamics of organizational change stand as one form of applicatory knowledge that colleges and universities undergoing change would find useful to administrative practice (Braxton, 2005). In some cases, such a conversion of knowledge to practical action requires knowledge of reliable ways for such a conversion to occur. In turn, reliable knowledge results from the replication of research. Braxton suggests a need for applicatory knowledge about such topics as organizational change, faculty personnel decisions, and faculty hiring decisions.

Interpretative professional knowledge springs from "wisdom and judgment" needed to make decisions of practice (Eraut, 1988). Braxton (2005) asserts that scholarship centered on the development of interpretative professional knowledge can delineate various perspectives on emerging issues confronting the various forms of administrative work in higher education such as the presidency, academic affairs administration, student affairs administration, admissions, and institutional advancement. Reviews of literature on such issues can add to the creation of interpretative professional knowledge (Braxton, 2005).

The graduate training of scholars to prepare them to make contributions to the three forms of professional knowledge in Level Two presents another issue of importance to the engagement of scholars of higher education and scholars of other academic fields of study. In Chapter 6, McDaniels and Skogsberg envision an expanded role for graduate education in the academic disciplines by outlining approaches to what they refer to as compelling awareness of, encouraging application, and engaging in the scholarship of practice. For example, they describe strategies designed to form an awareness of the scholarship of practice as well as strategies intended to develop the confidence and competence needed to engage in the scholarship of practice within and outside the student's own academic discipline. Moreover, McDaniels and Skogsberg present strategies to encourage graduate students to make contributions to the scholarship of practice.

We posit that these various strategies should focus specifically on graduate students' acquisition of knowledge, skills, and values to enable their engagement in the scholarship of practice. Put differently, these strategies should center attention on socializing graduate students to make contributions to replicative, applicatory, and interpretative professional knowledge.

Level Three of the Scholarship of Practice

As stated in Chapter 1, the third level of the scholarship of practice entails the use of replicative, applicatory, and interpretative forms of professional knowledge to develop a knowledge base for administrative work in higher education. Like Level Two of the scholarship of practice, such a knowledge base serves as a foundation for the stewardship of administrative practice as it provides a rational basis for administrative decision-making and action. Put differently, it safeguards administrative practice by moving it beyond action otherwise based upon less than sufficient types of knowledge. Higher education as a social institution also benefits from such a knowledge base.

The words *unknown* and *uncertain* best characterize the existence of an organized knowledge base for administrative work in higher education comprised of replicative, applicatory, and interpretative forms of professional knowledge. From the findings of Kramer and Braxton in Chapter 1, we know that almost 40% of the articles published during the past 20 years in the core journals of higher education made some contribution to these three forms of professional knowledge. However, the extent to which such knowledge assumes an organized form remains unknown. Taken together, these articles and future articles provide building blocks of an organized knowledge base for administrative work. However, some issues need attention before such integrative scholarship can take place.

As Kramer and Braxton argue in Chapter 1, such a knowledge base defies a unitary structure as administrative work in higher education consists of different segments of practice organized around different roles and functions such as the president, the chief academic officer, chief student affairs officer, institutional advancement director, and admissions officer (Braxton, 2005). Thus, distinct knowledge bases for each of these segments of administrative practice are necessary.

Nevertheless, some aspects of administrative work may apply to most, if not all, administrative segments. Moreover, as Kramer and Braxton point out in Chapter 1, such discrete knowledge bases consist of a range of topics critical to administrative practice (Braxton, 2005). Furthermore, each critical topical area requires in-depth coverage of it to guide administrative practice. Accordingly, Kramer and Braxton concluded that the attainment of Level Three of a scholarship of practice stands as "an elusive and lofty goal."

Engagement in the scholarship of integration offers an approach to the organizational work needed to move Level Three of a scholarship of practice forward. Boyer (1990) defines the scholarship of integration as "fitting one's own research or the research of others into larger intellectual patterns" (p. 19). Scholars of higher education could engage in the scholarship of integration using articles published in the core journals of higher education and other higher education-focused journals and publications that pertain to replicative, applicatory, and interpretative forms of professional knowledge. From such integrative scholarship, knowledge bases for administrative work might emerge.

Closing Thoughts

Each of the three levels of a scholarship of practice for higher education protect the welfare of individual colleges and universities and higher education as a social institution by assuring that institutional decision making and institutional action rest on a bedrock of empirical research and scholarship rather than on personal experience, commonsense, trial and error, and "back-pocket" thinking of institutional practitioners. Put differently, the scholarship of practice acts as a steward of higher education.

NEW DIRECTIONS FOR HIGHER EDUCATION • DOI: 10.1002/he

The formulations of this chapter describe each of the three levels of a scholarship of practice and their enactment. Level One of the scholarship of practice, or the use of empirical research to guide institutional policy and action, stands well within the grasp of institutional practitioners. However, engagement in Levels Two and Three depends on the scholarly or, in the case of public intellectuals, wider community. The viability of higher education as a social institution depends on the enactment of all three levels of a scholarship of practice.

References

Boyer E. L. (1990). *Scholarship reconsidered: Priorities for the professoriate*. Princeton, NJ: The Carnegie Foundation for the Advancement of Teaching.

Braxton, J. M. (2005). Reflections on a scholarship of practice. *The Review of Higher Education, 28*(2), 285–293.

Braxton, J. M., Doyle, W. R., Hartley, H. V., Hirschy, A. S., Jones, W. A. & McLendon, M. K. (2014). *Rethinking college student retention*. San Francisco, CA: Jossey-Bass.

Eraut, M. (1988). Knowledge creation and knowledge use in professional contexts. *Studies in Higher Education, 10*, 117–132.

Gasman, M. (Ed.). (2016). *Academics going public: How to write and speak beyond academe*. New York, NY: Routledge.

Gattone, C. (2006). *The social scientist as public intellectual: Critical reflections in a changing world*. Lanham, MD: Rowman and Littlefield.

Posner, R. A. (2001). *Public intellectuals: A study in decline*. Cambridge, MA: Harvard University Press.

Reason, R. D., & Kimball, E. W. (2012). A new theory-to-practice model for student affairs: Integrating scholarship, context, and reflection. *Journal of Student Affairs Research and Practice, 49*, 359–376.

St. John, E. P., McKinney, J. S., & Tuttle, T. (2006). Using action inquiry to address critical challenges. In E. P. St. John & M. Wilkerson (Eds.), *New directions for institutional research: No. 130, Reframing persistence research to improve academic success* (pp. 63–76). San Francisco, CA: Jossey-Bass.

Thapar, R. (2015). *The public intellectual in India*. New Delhi, India: Aleph BookCompany.

Wiseman, N. (2013). *The public intellectual in Canada*. Toronto, Canada: University of Toronto Press.

John M. Braxton is professor of education in the Higher Education Leadership and Policy Program at Peabody College of Vanderbilt University.

Todd C. Ream is professor of higher education at Taylor University and distinguished fellow with Excelsia College (New South Wales).

INDEX

103

NEW DIRECTIONS FOR HIGHER EDUCATION

ORDER FORM SUBSCRIPTION AND SINGLE ISSUES

DISCOUNTED BACK ISSUES:

Use this form to receive 20% off all back issues of *New Directions for Higher Education*.
All single issues priced at **$23.20** (normally $29.00)

TITLE	ISSUE NO.	ISBN

*Call 1-800-835-6770 or see mailing instructions below. When calling, mention the promotional code JBNND to receive
your discount. For a complete list of issues, please visit www.wiley.com/WileyCDA/WileyTitle/productCd-HE.html*

SUBSCRIPTIONS: (1 YEAR, 4 ISSUES)

☐ New Order   ☐ Renewal

U.S.	☐ Individual: $89	☐ Institutional: $356
CANADA/MEXICO	☐ Individual: $89	☐ Institutional: $398
ALL OTHERS	☐ Individual: $113	☐ Institutional: $434

*Call 1-800-835-6770 or see mailing and pricing instructions below.
Online subscriptions are available at www.onlinelibrary.wiley.com*

ORDER TOTALS:

Issue / Subscription Amount: $ _____

Shipping Amount: $ _____
(for single issues only – subscription prices include shipping)

Total Amount: $ _____

SHIPPING CHARGES:	
First Item	$6.00
Each Add'l Item	$2.00

*(No sales tax for U.S. subscriptions. Canadian residents, add GST for subscription orders. Individual rate subscriptions must
be paid by personal check or credit card. Individual rate subscriptions may not be resold as library copies.)*

BILLING & SHIPPING INFORMATION:

☐ **PAYMENT ENCLOSED:** *(U.S. check or money order only. All payments must be in U.S. dollars.)*

☐ **CREDIT CARD:**   ☐ VISA   ☐ MC   ☐ AMEX

Card number _____ Exp. Date _____

Card Holder Name _____ Card Issue # _____

Signature _____ Day Phone _____

☐ **BILL ME:** *(U.S. institutional orders only. Purchase order required.)*

Purchase order # _____
Federal Tax ID 13559302 • GST 89102-8052

Name _____

Address _____

Phone _____ E-mail _____

Copy or detach page and send to: **John Wiley & Sons, Inc. / Jossey Bass**
PO Box 55381
Boston, MA 02205-9850

PROMO JBNND